IMAGES OF WAR

US Naval Aviation
1898–1945

The Pioneering Years to the
Second World War

US Naval air power! Douglas SBD Dauntless dive-bombers of VB-4 ranged aboard the USS *Ranger* (CV-4) in 1943.

IMAGES OF WAR

US Naval Aviation 1898–1945

The Pioneering Years to the Second World War

RARE PHOTOGRAPHS FROM NAVAL ARCHIVES

LEO MARRIOTT

Pen & Sword
AVIATION

First published in Great Britain in 2021 by
PEN & SWORD AVIATION
An imprint of
Pen & Sword Books Ltd
Yorkshire – Philadelphia

ISBN 978 1 52678 539 8

A CIP catalogue record for this book is available from the British Library.

Typeset in 12/14.5 Gill Sans by SJmagic DESIGN SERVICES, India.

Printed and bound in England by CPI Group (UK) Ltd, Croydon, CR0 4YY.

Pen & Sword Books Ltd incorporates the imprints of Pen & Sword Archaeology, Atlas, Aviation, Battleground, Discovery, Family History, History, Maritime, Military, Naval, Politics, Social History, Transport, True Crime, Claymore Press, Frontline Books, Praetorian Press, Seaforth Publishing and White Owl.

For a complete list of Pen & Sword titles please contact

PEN & SWORD BOOKS LTD
47 Church Street, Barnsley, South Yorkshire, S70 2AS, England
E-mail: enquiries@pen-and-sword.co.uk
Website: www.pen-and-sword.co.uk

Or

PEN AND SWORD BOOKS
1950 Lawrence Rd, Havertown, PA 19083, USA
E-mail: Uspen-and-sword@casematepublishers.com
Website: www.penandswordbooks.com

Contents

Glossary and Abbreviations

AA	Anti-Aircraft
CAP	Combat Air Patrol
C-in-C	Commander-in-Chief
CVG	Carrier Air Group
DP	Dual-Purpose gun
HMS	His Majesty's Ship
NACA	National Advisory Council for Aeronautics
NAS	Naval Air Station
RAF	Royal Air Force
RNAS	Royal Navy Air Service
TF/TG	Task Force / Task Group
US	United States
USAAC	United States Army Air Corps
USAAF	United States Army Air Force
USAAS	United States Army Air Service
USMC	United States Marine Corps
USN	United Sates Navy
USS	United States Ship

US Navy ship designations: US Navy ships were (and still are) identified by a combination of letters indicating the ship's role followed by a sequential number for that type of ship. Role letters included BB (Battleship), CA and CL (Heavy and Light Cruisers) and DD (Destroyer). The first US aircraft carrier (USS *Langley*) was designated CV-1, the letters CV standing for Carrier – Heavier than Air (to distinguish it from ships designed to support airship operations), and subsequent carriers received sequential numbers. After the Second World War, the prefix was changed in some cases to reflect specialised roles, including CVS (anti-submarine carrier) and CVA (attack carrier). Designations for other classes of aircraft carrier included CVL (Light Aircraft Carrier) and CVE (Escort Carrier).

US Navy aircraft and squadron designations: In 1922, a system of aircraft designations was introduced which remained in place until 1962, when US Navy and USAF systems were merged. An aircraft type was designated by a system of letters and numbers that indicated the function or role, the model sequence number and the manufacturer. For example, the F2B was the second (2) Fighter (F) design by Boeing (B). Carrier-based aircraft roles were defined as Fighter (F), Bomber (B), Scout (S) or Observation (O). Sometimes these could be combined (e.g SB – Scout Bomber) or qualified (e.g. TB – Torpedo Bomber). In the case of the first design by a manufacturer, the numeric sequence number was omitted (e.g. the Boeing FB). The letters indicating the role or function were also applied to US Navy squadrons such as VF-5 (Fighting squadron 5) or VT-3 (Torpedo squadron 3). A supplementary letter might indicate an additional function, such as VF-3B, which also had a bombing role. USMC squadrons inserted an M after the number, for example, VF-3M, but later, in 1937, the M preceded the function letter (e.g. VMF-10). These aircraft and squadron designations are used throughout this book.

Introduction

In August 1945, off the coast of Japan, the US Navy was able to deploy the greatest naval force the world had ever seen. Its strength lay not in lines of towering battleships but in widely spread task forces, each centred on groups of four or more aircraft carriers. Although the Second World War was eventually brought to a dramatic end by the dropping of two atomic bombs, the carriers and aircraft of the US Navy had already completely destroyed or neutralised the once formidable Imperial Japanese Navy and were now pounding Japan itself in preparation for Operation Olympic – the invasion of the Japanese homeland, which fortunately became unnecessary when Japan surrendered on 15 August 1945. By that time the US Navy was established as the most powerful in the world, a position it retains to this day, again by virtue of its unequalled carrier air strength.

It is amazing to realise that this state of affairs in 1945 had been achieved in only forty-two years since the Wright brothers' first tentative flights and only

Entering service towards the end of the First World War, the Curtiss F-5L flying boat utilised a British-developed hull form and was the US Navy's standard patrol aircraft during most of the 1920s.

A line-up of newly delivered float-equipped Martin T3M-1 torpedo bombers in late 1926. This aircraft could be fitted with a conventional undercarriage for carrier operations and developed versions remained in service as late as 1937.

thirty-four years after the US Navy had obtained its first powered aircraft. The unfolding story of this rapid progress is illustrated by over 200 photos in this book, which start with the early pioneering efforts before and during the First World War and continue with the steady progress between the wars. In that period, the US Naval Aviation honed and refined the operation of increasingly sophisticated aircraft from the decks of its new carriers. In the Second World War, the US Navy was forced to rely on its aircraft carriers following the neutralisation of the battle fleet at Pearl Harbor on 7 December 1941. As it turned out, the carrier was now the major instrument of sea power, and over the next four years American industry built new carriers and aircraft at a rate the Axis powers could not match. For its part, the US Navy welded these new assets into formidable task forces, evolving and applying new tactics, and recruiting and training the sailors and airmen to the highest standards.

A major component of the carrier task forces that swept across the Pacific from 1943 until August 1945 were the new Essex class aircraft carriers. While these and the actions in which they participated are briefly described in this wide-ranging book, readers looking for more material relating to these magnificent ships are referred to the author's companion volume, *Essex Class Aircraft Carriers 1942–1991*, also published by Pen & Sword in the Images of War series.

The state of US naval air power in 1938 is well illustrated in the image of a Consolidated P2Y patrol flying boat over the carriers *Saratoga*, *Lexington* and *Langley* exercising off Hawaii.

The Grumman F4F Wildcat was the US Navy's front-line shipboard fighter from 1941 until mid-1943, when it was replaced by the F6F Hellcat. However, it remained in service in large numbers aboard the numerous escort carriers until the end of the war.

For the final assault against Japan, by August 1945 the US Pacific Fleet deployed at least ten Essex class carriers in addition to others commissioning or under repair. Each of these embarked an air group of about 100 modern aircraft such as the Vought F4U Corsair, seen here being marshalled forward to make space for other aircraft landing in turn.

Chapter 1

Pioneers of Naval Aviation

US naval interest in the possible military value of aviation can be traced back to 1898 when an inter-service committee was set up to investigate the potential of a flying machine, the Langley Aerodrome, which was then the subject of a government-sponsored development contract. Unfortunately, the Aerodrome failed to fly and although the Wright brothers successfully achieved the goal of manned powered controllable flight in December 1903, it was another five years before official US naval interest was to be reawakened. In 1908 the US Army arranged trials of the Wright Flyer and invited naval observers to attend. Subsequently, the Navy ordered two Curtiss flying machines, which were delivered in 1911, and also arranged for naval officers to train as pilots.

From this point progress was rapid. A Curtiss pilot, Eugene Ely, had already made the first take-off from a ship in November 1910 and subsequently the first landing aboard in January 1911. However, for the next few years, naval aviation concentrated on seaplanes and flying boats, and although the US Navy had pioneered the first steps in naval aviation, it was the British Royal Navy which then forged ahead under the pressure of war, and by 1918 it had the world's first flush-decked true aircraft carrier (HMS *Argus*). In addition, most capital ships were equipped with scout planes and fighters, which were flown off platforms erected over the gun turrets. The US Navy was quick to emulate this example, although their first aircraft carrier (USS *Langley*) did not commission until 1923.

During the First World War the aviation element of the US Navy in Europe was almost entirely dependent on its British, French and Italian allies for the supply of aircraft as well as airships. The US Navy Air Corps had been officially formed in 1915, but even by April 1917 it mustered only fifty-four aircraft and forty-eight pilots (including some still training). By November 1918 it had expanded dramatically, with 2,107 aircraft on strength together with fifteen dirigible airships. Personnel strength was 37,409 officers and men, with a further 2,462 US Marines on aviation duties. One field in which the US Navy was ahead of its allies was in the development of large flying boats. This was due to the work of Glenn Curtiss who, in 1914, had produced the Curtiss America, and developed versions were produced for the US Navy as the H-12 and H-16. After 1918, improved and redesigned variants were produced by the Naval Aircraft Factory as the PN series, some of which were still in service at the outbreak of the Second World War.

With peace restored, the US Navy used its flying boat experience to achieve the first aerial crossing of the Atlantic. It was flown in stages and not without some drama, but it served to publicise the capabilities of the naval air service at a time when the existence and role of naval air power was the subject of considerable debate.

In the late nineteenth century, the Secretary of the Smithsonian Institute, Samuel Langley, designed and built a number of powered model aerial vehicles for which he coined the term 'Aerodrome'. The success of these trials prompted the US Navy to take an interest and provide $50,000 for the development of a man-carrying aircraft and the full-scale Langley Aerodrome was ready for its first flight on 7 October 1903. It was launched from a catapult mounted atop a houseboat barge moored in the Potomac River, but failed to fly and flopped down into the river. A similar attempt on 8 December also failed and further work was abandoned, although in 1914 Glen Curtiss coaxed a modified version into the air for a few short hops, at least proving the soundness of Langley's original work.

A few days after Langley's second flight attempt, the Wright brothers made the now famous first manned flight in a powered controllable aircraft at Kittyhawk on 17 December 1903. However, it was not until 1907 that the US Army began to take an interest in their activities and organised a series of flight trials at Fort Myer, which commenced in the summer of 1908. Unfortunately, the Wright Flyer crashed on 17 September, killing the Army observer (Lieutenant Selfridge) and seriously injuring Orville Wright. The trials, which were observed by the US Navy, were successfully completed in 1909 with a new aeroplane.

On 14 November 1910, Eugene B. Ely, a civilian pilot employed by Glenn Curtiss, made the first take-off from a ship using a platform built over the bows of the cruiser USS *Birmingham* (the aircraft having previously been hoisted aboard by crane). A few weeks later, on 18 January 1911, he landed on the stern platform aboard the cruiser US *Pittsburgh*, anchored off Hunters Point, San Francisco Bay. He subsequently took off again (the moment captured in this photograph) and flew back to Selfridge Field. This was a convincing demonstration of the potential of the new aeroplanes for naval purposes.

Above: A view of the armoured cruiser USS *Pittsburgh* in January 1911 showing the temporary flight deck erected on the stern in preparation for Ely's flight trials. Not yet installed at this point was a system of arrester wires attached to sandbags arranged along each side of the deck.

Opposite above: Although the initial shipborne trials were flown by a civilian pilot, Glenn Curtiss had already offered to train two naval officers. The first of these was Lieutenant Theodore G. Ellyson USN, who reported to North Island, San Diego, at the end of 1910 and subsequently qualified as Naval Aviator No. 1. In this image, taken on 3 July 1911, he is shown at the controls of the A1 preparing for a flight with Captain Washington I. Chambers USN, who at that time was the senior naval officer responsible for aviation affairs.

Opposite below: The success of the military trials at Fort Myer and Ely's shipborne flights encouraged the US Navy to order aircraft, and although it subsequently bought a few Wright Model seaplanes in 1912, its first aircraft was actually a Curtiss pusher seaplane designated A-1 (later AH-1), which it acquired in July 1911.

Above: From 1911 to 1914, the US Navy purchased a total of fourteen Curtiss pusher aircraft given designations with the suffix A (landplanes) or AH (hydroplanes). These all featured the same basic biplane configuration with various engines (50–75hp) driving a pusher propeller, but there were detailed differences between individual aircraft. For example, AH-3, shown here being prepared for hoisting aboard a cruiser, no longer has a forward elevator, which was a feature of the earlier examples.

Opposite above: In April 1914, US Naval forces were instructed to occupy the Mexican port of Vera Cruz with the aim of preventing the landing of an arms shipment to insurgent forces that had previously staged a coup d'état against the constitutional government. Amongst the US warships present was the battleship USS *Mississippi* (BB-23), with the hydroplane AH-3 and an AB-3 (a Curtiss Type C) flying boat. The first operational mission flown by any US military aircraft occurred on 25 April, when Lieutenant Junior Grade Patrick Bellinger flew AB-3 on a reconnaissance mission over the harbour looking for reported mines.

Opposite below: A significant event occurred on 3 November 1915 when a Curtiss F flying boat, piloted by Lieutenant Commander Henry C. Mustin, was catapulted into the air from the stern of the armoured cruiser USS *North Carolina* off the Florida coast at Pensacola. The catapult mechanism, operated by compressed air, had previously been tested successfully at the Washington Navy Yard as early as 1912 and the shipborne trial was the first time it had been tried at sea. The AB-3 is here mounted on the catapult during subsequent trials. *BPL*

Opposite above: A detailed view of the catapult structure installed aboard the USS *North Carolina*. On the central track can be seen a trolley on which the aircraft could be mounted, having been hoisted aboard by crane. Tracks on either side of the mast hold trolleys on which other aircraft could be stowed. However, the whole arrangement was fixed and interfered with the normal running of the ship, and also limited the use of the after 8-in gun mounting, so it was only applied to two other ships (the cruisers USS *Seattle* and USS *Huntingdon*) and was removed from all three in 1917 when America entered the war.

Opposite below: Although the majority of the aircraft procured in the first few years were of Curtiss designs, the US Navy showed an early willingness to investigate other aircraft that embodied advanced thinking. One such was the British tailless Dunne design, which featured sharply swept wings, this configuration being intended to offer exceptional longitudinal stability. Two examples, designated AH-7 and AH-10 (the latter shown here), were built under licence by the Burgess Company of Marblehead MA and delivered in 1916. Although no further orders were forthcoming, the stable flight characteristics of these aircraft rendered them suitable for a series of aerial gunnery tests – the first conducted by the US Navy.

Following the American declaration of war against Germany, the US Navy began sending detachments of personnel to France. At that time the Navy had few suitable aircraft of its own and relied heavily on Britain and France to provide suitable machines. This is a French Tellier T.3 flying boat, one of thirty-four eventually transferred to the US Navy, based at Le Croisic (near St Nazaire). On 22 November, Ensign Kenneth R. Smith USNRF, piloting a T.3, made the first operational armed patrol by a US Navy crew, searching for reported German U-boats off Belle Île.

Above: In addition to providing aircraft and bases, both France and Britain also made arrangements to train US Navy personnel, including ab initio training for pilots. This Caudron GIII-E2 was used for flying training at Tours, where the first detachment of US Navy trainee pilots was sent in 1917. *NHIC*

Opposite above: The first American-designed and built aircraft to join US Navy units in France was the Curtiss HS-1 flying boat. Larger than the earlier F boat, the HS-1L was powered by an American-built 350hp Liberty engine, carried a crew of two or three and could be armed with two 180lb depth charges.

Opposite below: It was soon found that the 180lb depth charges were ineffective and the HS-1L was modified by extending the wingspan by 12 feet so that it could carry a pair of 230lb depth charges. The modified aircraft were designated HS-2L and a total of 182 HS-1L and HS-2L flying boats were sent to units in France, although most of these were the unmodified HS-1L. They were used for coastal patrols over the English Channel as well as the French Mediterranean and Atlantic coasts. The increased wingspan of the HS-2L is readily apparent in this view.

Opposite above: The rapid growth of US naval aviation during the First World War period is illustrated by this view of seaplanes lined up at Pensacola FL in 1918. In the foreground are Curtiss H-16 flying boats, a development of the original Curtiss America which spawned the H series, of which the H-12 and H-16 were the most significant. Curtiss produced 184 H-16s (including sixty supplied in kit form to the RNAS) while the Naval Aircraft Factory built another 150. In Britain, an improved version known as the Felixstowe F-5L was produced and this in turn was also built in the US and Canada, a total of 227 being delivered. In the background a pair of HS-1L flying boats can be seen at anchor. *NHIC*

Opposite below: A close-up view of an H-16 flying boat armed with a pair of 230lb bombs. In US Navy service the H-16 was powered by a pair of 400hp Liberty engines and carried a crew of four. Noticeable in this head-on view are the flared hull sponsons, which were necessary to counter the nose-down pitch moment produced by the high-mounted engines at full power for take-off.

Impressed by operations of the RAF's Independent Force equipped with Handley Page O/400 heavy bombers, the US Navy determined to set up its own strategic bomber force, which became the Northern Bombing Group. In the summer of 1918, crews were sent to train with RAF bomber squadrons and subsequently, Squadron 1 of the US Navy began operations with a night raid against the German U-boat base at Ostend. The aircraft used were Italian-built Caproni Ca.44 three-engined bombers, which featured a unique twin-boom layout, the third engine being mounted in the rear of the centre fuselage driving a pusher propeller. A total of nineteen Caproni bombers were acquired by the US Navy.

Above: By 1918, the capital ships of the Royal Navy's Grand Fleet embarked about 100 aircraft made up of single-seat fighters and two-seat observation seaplanes. Aboard battleships, the fighters were flown off platforms built over the roof of a gun turret and after the war the idea was adopted by the US Navy, which proposed so equipping eight battleships. The first of these was USS *Texas* (BB-35), shown here with a British Sopwith Camel fighter on the flight platform over B turret. The first flight from the platform was made by Lieutenant Commander Edward McDonnell USN on 9 March 1919.

Opposite above: Plans to equip eight battleships, each with two platforms (on B and X turrets), were not fully implemented and the equipment was removed from all in 1921. This was because the platforms interfered with the operation of the guns and the aircraft mounted thereon interfered with the view from the ship's bridge. Also, the US Navy was then developing a new and more flexible catapult system. Flying off from the platforms was a hazardous business at the best of times, as shown by this Sopwith 1½ Strutter taking off (probably from USS *Oklahoma* BB37). After leaving the platform the pilot is diving down to pick up speed before (hopefully) climbing away.

Opposite below: In 1917, the US Navy investigated the possibility of aeroplanes flying across the Atlantic to Europe under their own power rather than being delivered by ship. This led to the development of the NC (Navy Curtiss) series of flying boats, of which four were allocated to a transatlantic attempt in 1919 after the war had ended. In the event, only NC-4 completed the 3,925-mile flight, staging from Newfoundland through the Azores and Lisbon before reaching Plymouth on 31 May, where she is shown resting at anchor. The US Navy gained considerable international prestige from having accomplished the first transatlantic crossing by an aeroplane.

Some of the NC flying boat crews pose with naval officials on 2 July 1919 after their return to the US. In the front row (from left to right) are Lieutenant Commander A.C. Read, pilot of NC-4; Josephus Daniels, Secretary of the Navy; Commander John H. Towers, pilot of NC-3; Franklin D. Roosevelt, then Assistant Secretary of the Navy; and Lieutenant Commander P. Bellinger, pilot of NC-1. *NHIC*

Chapter 2

The Navy's First
Aircraft Carriers

After the end of the First World War there were widespread cutbacks in naval strength, but the importance of naval aviation had been established and by 1920 it still retained about 850 aircraft and thirty airships. A significant step in 1921 was the establishment of a Bureau of Aeronautics (BuAer), responsible to the Secretary of the Navy for all aviation affairs. This gave the US Navy complete control over the specification and production of its aircraft and their operation, as well as recruitment and training of its personnel.

It was not until 1922 that the US Navy at last had an aircraft carrier with a full-length flight deck in the form of the 12,700-ton USS Langley (designated CV-1). Although by later standards a relatively small carrier and her speed of only 14 knots precluded her operating directly with the fleet, for the next five years she was a valuable test bed for the application of new aircraft handling techniques, evaluation of new aircraft and the development of operational tactics. In 1921, the world's major navies had met in an attempt to halt the massively expensive naval arms race that followed end of the war in 1918. The outcome was the 1922 Washington Naval Treaty, which resulted in the scrapping of dozens of obsolete warships, cancelling others under construction, and setting limits on any new construction. In particular, the treaty limited the US (and Great Britain) to a maximum of 135,000 tons of aircraft carrier construction, while individual carriers should not exceed 27,000 tons. These limitations directly shaped US carrier construction programmes until 1937, by which time the various treaties had expired.

One outcome of the Washington Treaty was that the US, Great Britain and Japan were permitted to convert various large battlecruisers then under construction to be completed as aircraft carriers, and these were exempted from the 27,000-ton limit. This resulted in the US Navy obtaining two large and fast carriers in the shape of the USS Lexington (CV-2) and USS Saratoga (CV-3), both of which commissioned at the end of 1927 and ushered in a new era of US carrier operations. With a speed of 33 knots, they were by far the fastest major warships in the fleet, and on a standard displacement of around 39,000 tons, they could accommodate and operate an air group of eighty aircraft. Almost immediately, they participated in major fleet exercises, demonstrating that a new era of naval warfare was dawning.

Above: Having observed British progress in developing aircraft carriers during the First World War, the US Navy was eager to commission one for itself. To speed up the process, and to reduce costs, the fleet collier USS *Jupiter* was selected for conversion. Originally commissioned in April 1913, the *Jupiter* was the first ship in the fleet to feature a turbo electric propulsion system. Decommissioned on 24 March 1920, work then began at the Norfolk Naval Shipyard VA to convert her into an aircraft carrier and she was renamed USS *Langley* (CV-1) on 11 April 1920. *NHIC*

Opposite above: This sketch dated 1919 shows the salient points of the USS *Langley* as it would be converted to an aircraft carrier. All the derricks and king posts associated with handling coal have been removed and replaced with an open structure carrying a full-length flight deck over the original bridge and wheelhouse, which is retained, and stretching to the stern over the after superstructure. The USS *Jupiter* had featured twin funnels, one on either beam, and in the conversion the starboard funnel was ducted below the flight deck to vent on the port side.

Opposite below: The USS *Langley* eventually commissioned on 20 March 1922 as the US Navy's first aircraft carrier. This view, showing her as completed, was taken in the following December and the lines of the original collier's hull are plainly evident. Immediately below the aircraft on deck (an Aeromarine 39B) can be seen the casing covering the ducts of the port side funnel. In the background is a C-Series blimp, at that time operated by the US Army for coastal patrols.

Above: Aircraft handling arrangements aboard the USS *Langley* were a direct result of the nature of the ship's conversion. There was no conventional hangar but four out of the original six holds were used to stow aircraft. These were arranged in pairs with the hold space between them utilised as a bay for the lift well while the sixth hold, right forward, became an aviation fuel bunker, holding a total of 578 tons. Aircraft were lifted from the holds by means of two overhead gantry cranes and placed on what was originally the collier's weather deck, which was used for aircraft maintenance and stowage, as shown here. While it was covered over, it was open at the sides apart from the girder structure supporting the flight deck. The single lift, situated amidships, then carried aircraft up to the flight deck. The holds could accommodate thirty-four aircraft or up to fifty-five if in a dismantled state.

Opposite above: On 17 October 1922, flying an Aeromarine 39-B, Lieutenant Commander G. de Chevalier (Naval Aviator No. 7) is about to make the first landing on *Langley*'s flight deck. Below the undercarriage axle are a row of hooks designed to catch longitudinal wires stretching along the flight deck, the idea being that they will prevent the aircraft sliding across the deck and over the side. However, in a belt and braces situation, the aircraft is also equipped with a trailing arrester hook, which should catch a series of transverse wires, although braking action was crudely supplied by weighted bags attached to the wires. In time, a more sophisticated system of arrester wires was fitted and the longitudinal wires were removed by the end of the decade.

Opposite below: An Aeromarine 39-B being hoisted aboard the *Langley*. One hundred and fifty of these aircraft were ordered in 1917, the largest single order for a US Navy aircraft up to that time. Of these, 100 were built as A39-B two-seat trainers, and several of these were used for land-based trials on a dummy carrier deck at Naval Air Station (NAS) Langley, Virginia. The gooseneck crane being used here was one of two (situated port and starboard); they were also used for handling the seaplanes that formed part of the aircraft complement.

Opposite above: The process of hoisting seaplanes on and off ships was a cumbersome business that entailed the parent ship having to heave to while the operation was conducted. Consequently, the US Navy developed a compact trainable catapult (Type A Mark 1) in which the acceleration was provided by compressed air and could be operated while the ship was underway. In addition, techniques were developed whereby the aircraft could be recovered while the ship was moving. After successful trials in 1922 aboard the USS *Maryland* (BB-46), similar catapults were installed on the quarterdeck of another eleven battleships including USS *Oklahoma* (BB-37), shown here in December 1922. The aircraft being prepared for launching is a Vought VE-7H two-seat observation seaplane.

Opposite below: In 1916 it was decided that the British de Havilland DH.4 bomber would be adapted for mass production in the US and would be powered by the new 400hp Liberty engine. It subsequently became the only American-produced landplane to see service with US Navy services in Europe before the end of hostilities in November 1918. After the war, the US Navy received no fewer than 170 DH.4Bs, either transferred from the US Army or built from surplus components by the Naval Aircraft Factory. Almost all were used as land-based observation aircraft or day bombers, and later as trainers and for general duties. The aircraft shown here was a unique conversion to the air ambulance role as a DH.4Amb-1, but it was written off in an accident on 22 May 1922 at San Diego.

Although the USS *Langley* was the US Navy's first aircraft carrier, it wasn't the Navy's first dedicated aviation ship. The USS *Aroostook* was a coastal passenger steamer built in 1907 but requisitioned in 1917 and converted into a minelayer. In 1919 she was taken in hand for conversion to an aviation support ship, a process that involved the removal of the mine rails to provide an open space at the stern, the installation of booms and derricks for hoisting aircraft, and the provision of aircraft maintenance and repair facilities. As such, she played an important role in supporting the Curtiss NC flying boats in their attempted transatlantic flights (see Ch.1) and subsequently remained in service until 1931. In this mid-1920s image she has a PN flying boat secured on the after deck.

Above: The PN series of twin-engined flying boats were developed by the Naval Aircraft Factory. The PN-5 and PN-6 were actually new designations for the Curtiss F-5L, which continued in production after 1918. However, the PN-7, while utilising the same hull, was fitted with stronger and lighter metal-framed wings and more powerful Wright T-2 engines. It was succeeded by the PN-8 with a metal hull and Packard V-12 engines, and a modified version, the PN-9, was used for an attempt to fly from San Francisco to Hawaii but was forced down some 560 miles short of the islands. Amazingly, the crew completed the trip under jury-rigged sails! The last pair of PN-10s were completed as the PN-12, the main difference being the installation of more reliable air-cooled radial engines. This is the Wright Cyclone powered PN-12, which flew in 1927, and the following year, together with its Pratt & Whitney powered sister ship, established a number of speed, duration and payload records. It is shown in 1928 over a section of the US Navy reserve fleet at San Diego, where a staggering number of destroyers are laid up.

Opposite above: Another early aviation ship was the USS *Wright*, which commissioned on 16 December 1921, nominally as a 'lighter-than-air aircraft tender' designated AZ-1. However, she was employed almost exclusively as a tender to seaplanes and also the large patrol flying boats, which assumed an increasingly important role. Consequently, in 1925 she was reclassified as a seaplane tender (AV-1) and for the rest of the decade served as the flagship of the Air Squadron, Scouting Fleet. She is shown here at that time with a Vought O2U observation seaplane stowed on the after deck. In fact, she had a long and varied career and was not finally decommissioned until June 1946.

From the early days, the US Navy recognised the potential of torpedo-carrying aircraft and the Curtiss CS was produced to meet this requirement. Powered by a 525hp Wright T-2 inline liquid-cooled engine, it accommodated a crew of three and could carry a 1,618lb torpedo under the central fuselage. The prototype CS-1 flew in late 1923 but although the aircraft performed well, US Navy policy was to put production contracts out to tender. The result was that the Glenn Martin company obtained contracts for a total of seventy-five aircraft designated as SC-1 and SC-2, which entered service from 1925 onwards. It was produced in both land plane and seaplane versions and was also used as a bomber and scout aircraft. Despite this flexibility, its front-line career was short and all had been withdrawn by 1928.

Opposite above: The flat expanse at the north end of the Coronado peninsula, which encloses San Diego Bay, was used for aviation purposes as early as 1911 when Glenn Curtiss set up a flying school. It was here that many of the early naval aviators first learned to fly and in 1912, the US Navy briefly operated an air station, although the Navy did not establish a permanent presence as NAS North Island until 1917. In the meantime, in 1913, the US Army had set up its own establishment named Rockwell Field, which remained in being until 1937. In this 1924 photo, which looks to the west, the naval facilities are on the right (north) side of the grass landing strips and in the foreground, while the Army camp is on the left (south side).

Opposite below: In the 1920s the US Navy actively participated in air races and record attempts as a means of encouraging improvements in aircraft and engine performance, and also for the publicity value, which helped in gaining support in the ongoing competition with the US Army for the limited financial resources available. In 1920, the US Army had won the prestigious Pulitzer Trophy Race and this prompted the Navy to order a pair of racing aircraft from Curtiss. These became the CR-1 and CR-2 (CR – Curtiss Racer) but in the 1922 race the Navy could only come in behind two Army Curtiss R-6s. The photo shows Lieutenant H.J. Brow USN alongside the CR-2, which was placed third. However, this aircraft was converted to a CR-3 seaplane and won the 1923 Schneider Trophy races held over the Solent, England, at a speed of 177.4mph.

The Omaha class light cruisers, which entered service from 1923 to 1925, were the first US Navy warships to be completed with facilities for carrying and launching seaplanes. Initially, these were a pair of Vought VE-9s which were carried on deck in a space between the after funnel and the mainmast, and were hoisted out by crane for a water take-off. In 1927, the USS *Memphis* (CL-13), shown here, was fitted with a pair of Type A Mk.III trainable catapults and the remaining nine ships of the class were subsequently also modified. A Vought OU-1 has just been launched from the starboard catapult.

Opposite above: The Curtiss CS described earlier was also built by the Martin company as the SC-1 at their Cleveland factory, and they used this experience to produce the Martin T3M/T4M series of torpedo bombers. Entering service in 1928, the T4M (shown here) served with VT-1B aboard the USS *Lexington* (CV-2) and VT-2B aboard the USS *Saratoga* (CV-3), and some examples remained in service with Reserve squadrons as late as 1937.

Opposite below: Laid down as a battlecruiser in 1921 and launched on 3 October 1925, the USS *Lexington* (CV-2) commissioned as an aircraft carrier on 14 December 1927. This view shows her in the final stages of fitting out in October 1927 and the forward 8-in gun turrets are prominent in the foreground. The outstanding visual feature of these ships as converted was the massive funnel into which were trunked the uptakes from the sixteen boilers that provided the steam to the General Electric turbo-electric machinery driving four shafts. Power output was 180,000shp, making them the most powerful warships in the world and enabling speeds of over 33 knots to be achieved.

USS *Lexington* makes a fine impression as she runs at full speed during her post-completion trials, and the lines of the original battlecruiser hull are clearly evident. With a speed of 33 knots and carrying a complement of up to eighty aircraft, they were the fastest and most powerful aircraft carriers in the world. However, the 8-in guns, which took up valuable deck space, had been incorporated as it was thought that the carrier might have to fight off enemy destroyers and cruisers. In practice, this never happened as war experience showed that carriers operated well away from opposing surface forces, their means of attack and defence resting with the embarked aircraft.

Opposite above: The other converted battlecruiser to commission as an aircraft carrier was the USS *Saratoga* (CV-3), which was launched on 7 April 1925 and commissioned on 16 November 1927, a month before her sister ship *Lexington*. The following year, both carriers deployed to San Pedro (near Long Beach, CA), where they were based while working up the ship's crews and air squadrons. In this view taken at that time, *Saratoga* has the Martin T4M-1 torpedo bombers of VT-2B ranged on deck, with one just airborne over the bows.

Opposite below: Due to their identical appearance, a certain amount of confusion arose over identification, and by the start of 1929, a broad black vertical stripe was applied to *Saratoga*'s funnel to assist in this respect. This is clearly shown in this view of Puget Sound Naval Yard in late 1929, where the US Navy's entire carrier fleet is alongside. In the centre is *Saratoga*, carrying the funnel strip, with *Lexington* behind. In the foreground is the USS *Langley*, and its relatively small size in comparison to the two new carriers is evident. *NHIC*

Despite its small size, the *Langley* proved invaluable in developing operational methods and tactics that could be applied when the larger carriers entered service. This 1928 view of USS *Langley* shows just how advanced US naval aviation was by that time. There are thirty-three aircraft shown, including one floatplane at the stern. Indeed, the *Langley*'s standard complement was intended to be twelve pursuit aircraft (fighters), twelve scouts and ten torpedo bombers (some of the latter being floatplanes), which compared favourably with the Royal Navy's contemporary and much larger HMS *Courageous*, which nominally could accommodate forty-eight aircraft, although it was rare for the British carrier ever to embark even half of its capacity.

Opposite: The size of the newly commissioned *Lexington* and *Saratoga* enabled a substantial air group to be embarked, as this view of *Lexington* in 1929 shows. Ranged in the foreground are Boeing F3B and Curtiss F6C fighters (powered by radial and in-line engines respectively) while at least a dozen Martin T4M torpedo bombers of VT-1B are further aft. In that year both carriers participated in Fleet Exercise IX and aircraft from *Saratoga* successfully simulated an attack on the Panama Canal, evading the fighters from *Lexington*. *NHIC*

In the 1920s and 1930s, Boeing were very much in the fighter business, supplying both the US Army and Navy with a series of nimble biplane fighters. The first was the Boeing FB, which produced in a number of variants, but all were powered by in-line water-cooled engines. By the late 1920s, the US Navy had decided that future carrier-based aircraft should be powered by air-cooled radial engines and Boeing therefore produced the F2B-1 powered by a 450hp Pratt & Whitney R-1340B. Deliveries began in January 1928 and all were allocated to VF-1B and VB-2B aboard the USS *Saratoga*, where they are shown ranged on deck during fleet exercises later that year (VB-2B was previously VF-6B and the aircraft still display that unit's numbering). *NHIC*

Chapter 3

Coming of Age

The 1930s was a decade of tremendous progress for US Naval Aviation, not least in the expansion of its carrier fleet. For most of the period, the *Lexington* and *Saratoga* provided the main element of the fleet's air power, but in 1934 they were joined by the USS *Ranger* (CV-4). As a clean-sheet design it introduced a number of new features, although not all were successful. With the Washington Treaty limitations in mind she was designed around a maximum standard displacement of 14,000 tons, which would then allow the construction of four more similar carriers. However, by 1934 the idea of building small carriers was abandoned and design of two larger, 20,000-ton carriers was begun. These were the Yorktown class, which commissioned in 1937 and 1938, and could each accommodate up to ninety-six aircraft. To remain within the treaty limits, a third carrier (USS *Wasp* CV-7) was laid down in 1936 on a reduced displacement of 15,000 tons but, like *Ranger*, she suffered from compromises made necessary by the reduced tonnage. A third Yorktown class was ordered when the provisions of the Washington and London treaties had lapsed in 1937. This was the USS *Hornet* (CV-8), but she was not completed until 1941 and is covered in Chapter 5.

In terms of aircraft, in 1930 the US Navy mustered a total of 1,081, of which, 664 were actual combat aircraft (the remainder included transports and trainers). By 1939 these figures had doubled to a total of 2,098, which included 1,316 combat aircraft. It should be noted that the combat aircraft figure included not only carrier-capable aircraft but also observation and scout floatplanes aboard battleships and cruisers, as well as flying boats. A decade of aircraft development also saw a substantial improvement in performance and operational capabilities. By the end of the 1930s the superiority of the monoplane was accepted and the first to enter naval service, in October 1937, was the Douglas TBD Devastator torpedo bomber. This was shortly followed by the Vought SB2U Vindicator scout bomber and both types gradually replaced their biplane predecessors. The replacement of biplane fighters took a little longer as conservative opinion favoured that configuration for its strength and manoeuvrability. In the event, the only monoplane fighter to reach the fleet in the 1930s was the Brewster F2A Buffalo, some of which were delivered at the close of 1939. It had won a selection contest against the rival Grumman XF4F-2, but after a short career, it lost out to a much improved version of the Grumman fighter.

Throughout the 1930s, a series of annual exercises known as Fleet Problems enabled US Naval Aviation to reach a high standard of proficiency and develop methods of operation and tactics that would stand it in good stead when war came in 1941. In particular, the carrier crews became adept at the handling of large numbers of aircraft, both in rapidly launching formations and then recovering them in the shortest possible time. Reports of the numbers of aircraft involved and the tempo of the flight deck operations were received with some incredulity, even scepticism, by foreign observers, notably the Royal Navy, whose own efficiency in carrier operations was nowhere near the reported US levels. As it transpired, only the Japanese Navy was able to match the progress of the US Navy.

The US Navy's first purpose-built aircraft carrier was the USS *Ranger* (CV-4), which was laid down at Newport News, VA, on 26 September 1931 and is seen here just after being launched on 25 February 1933. The original design was for a flush flight deck similar to the USS *Langley* but an island superstructure was added during the fitting-out process. Note the openings for the two centrally located aircraft lifts. Despite a displacement of only 14,000 tons, less than half that of the *Lexington* and *Saratoga*, she was intended to accommodate a similar sized air group of seventy-six aircraft as the clean-sheet design was able to prioritise on those features that facilitated the stowage and operation aircraft.

Above: The USS *Ranger* undergoing sea trials shortly after commissioning on 4 July 1934. A small island superstructure has been erected on the starboard side of the flight deck and this photo also shows the unusual funnel arrangement. The boiler uptakes were fed to six funnels, three situated well aft on either side of the flight deck, which could be lowered to the horizontal position during flying operations – an arrangement that did not prove satisfactory in practice and was not repeated in subsequent carrier designs.

Opposite above: A view of USS *Ranger* anchored at Colon in the Panama Canal Zone in 1935. *Ranger's* planned air group was made up of thirty-six dive and torpedo bombers, thirty-six pursuit aircraft (fighters), and four utility aircraft, and here some of the Great Lakes BG-1 dive-bombers operated by VB-3B are ranged on deck. Based on San Diego, the carrier remained in the Pacific for four years until January 1939, when she passed through the Panama Canal bound for exercise in the Caribbean. Thereafter she was based at Norfolk VA and operated in the Atlantic.

Opposite below: Dive-bomber squadron VB-3B was the only front-line US Navy squadron to be equipped the Great Lakes BG-1, receiving its first aircraft in October 1934 and continuing to fly them until 1938. Powered by a 750hp Pratt & Whitney R-1535 Wasp radial engine, the BG-1 had a range of 549 miles while carrying a single 1,000lb bomb. A total of sixty were delivered but over half of these were allocated to Marine squadrons VB-4M and VB-6M, and one of the latter's is shown here.

Opposite above: The Great Lakes Aircraft Corporation was one of the lesser known American aircraft manufacturers and was formed in 1928 when it took over the Martin factory at Cleveland after that company had transferred its activities to Baltimore. Great Lakes received contracts to build versions of the Martin T3M/T4M torpedo bomber, which were produced as the TG-1 and TG-2, the latter having more powerful 620hp Wright Cyclone R-1820 engines, and thirty-two of these were delivered beginning in 1930. Again, only a single squadron (VT-2) received this type and a formation of their aircraft is shown near San Diego in this photo dated July 1932.

Opposite below: In the early 1930s Boeing continued to improve the F2B and F3B fighters, and the result was the F4B, which, although superficially similar to its predecessors, introduced many detailed improvements. These included redesigned parallel-chord wings and a shorter, deeper fuselage. Although powered by the same 450hp Pratt & Whitney engine, top speed rose to 176mph as against 157mph for the F3B-1. The ultimate version was the F4B-4 shown here, which had a 550hp engine enclosed in a ring cowling and was capable of 188mph. Deliveries of the latter began in July 1932 and this section of three aircraft is from VF-3B, which at that time was based aboard the USS *Langley*. The F4B-4 remained in front-line service until 1938.

The Grumman Aircraft Engineering Corporation was formed in 1929 and two years later won a contract to provide the US Navy with a shipborne two-seat fighter. The result was the XFF-1 prototype shown here, which first flew on 29 December 1931. An advanced design for the time, it featured a retractable undercarriage (the first for a US Navy aircraft) and a fully enclosed cockpit for the two crew. Initially it was powered by a 616hp Wright R-1850E but this was subsequently replaced by a 750hp R-1820F, which resulted in a top speed of just over 200mph. This was faster than any of the current Navy single-seat fighters and consequently, twenty-seven FF-1s were ordered as well as thirty-three SF-1 scout versions. The fighters entered service with VF-5B aboard the USS *Lexington* in June 1933.

Opposite above: The success of the Grumman FF-1 began a period of over forty years when the company became the prime supplier of fighters to the US Navy. A logical development of the FF-1 was the slightly smaller and lighter single-seat XF2F-1, which, unsurprisingly, was a better performer with a top speed of 231mph. First flown in October 1933, the prototype was followed by fifty-four production F2F-1s, which reached squadrons aboard the USS *Lexington* (VF-2B) and USS *Ranger* (VF-3B) in 1935. VF-3B later transferred to the USS *Yorktown* and was redesignated VF-5. One of its aircraft is shown here, the code 5-F-1 indicating that it was the lead aircraft of Fighting Squadron 5.

Opposite below: The further development of the Grumman biplane fighters was the F3F-1, which featured a longer fuselage and increased wingspan to improve manoeuvrability. Fifty-four examples were ordered and they entered service in 1936. This F3F-1 based aboard the USS *Ranger* (CV-4) in January 1939 vividly displays the colourful range of markings carried by US Navy operational units in the 1930s. The tail colour indicates which carrier the aircraft is from (willow green for USS *Ranger*) and the fuselage band the three-plane section to which it is allocated (blue for Section 3). The cowling of the section leader's aircraft was painted in the same colour (blue) as the fuselage band while the other aircraft in the section (4-F-8 and 4-F-9) would have the top half or lower half of the cowling respectively in the same colour.

Until the advent of more modern aircraft carriers, *Saratoga* and *Lexington* provided the core air striking power of the US Navy. This is *Saratoga* in May 1933 with a representative selection of aircraft types of that era ranged on deck. These include some twenty Vought O3U-2 (later redesignated SU-1) observation/scout aircraft belonging to Marine squadron VC-14M, which was one of only two USMC squadrons to serve aboard a carrier until the outbreak of the Second World War (the other was VS-15M aboard *Lexington*). Ranged behind them are two dozen Boeing F4B-3 fighters of VF-1B and several Martin/Great Lakes TG-2 torpedo bombers.

Opposite above: *Saratoga*'s air group looks even more impressive when spread out ashore, in this case at NAS North Island, San Diego, in 1932. In the foreground are the Vought O3U-2s of VS-2 and at top left are the Boeing F3B-1s of VB-2B (a fighter squadron despite the VB-Bomber designation). To the right of them are them are the Great Lakes TG-2 torpedo bombers of VT-2B. Also in the picture, behind *Saratoga*'s O3Us are more Vought O3U-2s, which belong to VS-1B assigned to the USS *Langley* (CV-1).

Opposite below: In the 1920s the US Navy adopted the concept of the dive-bomber to supplement the torpedo bomber as a means of attacking enemy ships. Most of the early dive-bombers were adapted fighters such as the Curtiss F8C Helldiver developed in 1929. However, the Navy's first purpose-designed dive-bomber was the Martin T5M-1, which flew in prototype form in March 1930, but the subsequent production aircraft that entered service from 1932 were designated BM-1 or BM-2. This impressive formation, flown by BM-2s of VT-1S based aboard the USS *Lexington*, dates from January 1934. A total of thirty-three aircraft were delivered (sixteen BM-1, sixteen BM-2 and a single XBM-1 allocated to NACA for test purposes) but were retired from front-line service in 1937, although several examples were used for various purposes by shore units until 1940.

Although nominally designated as a dive-bomber, the Martin BM-2 could also carry a single torpedo and was often allocated that role (as evidenced by the designation of VT-1S as a torpedo bomber squadron). Until well into the Second World War, US carriers were equipped to operate aircraft while going astern, a manoeuvre that was regularly exercised although seldom used in practice, and this BM-2 about to take off over the stern of USS *Lexington* in May 1934 has attracted a substantial audience.

Above: The 14,000-ton USS *Ranger* (CV-4) was originally intended as the lead ship of a class of five similar carriers. However, even before *Ranger* was launched, her limitations were recognised and consequently orders were placed instead for two larger 20,000-ton carriers. These were the Yorktown class and the lead ship was laid down on 24 May 1934, launched on 4 April 1936 and commissioned on 30 September 1937. USS *Yorktown* (CV-5) is shown here running trials in November 1937. Her flight deck was served by three lifts, and with a length of 802 feet was almost 100 feet longer than *Ranger*'s. With a nominal air group on ninety-six aircraft, she was a formidable addition to the fleet.

Opposite: An aerial view of the USS *Yorktown* at anchor in January 1938. The symmetrical deck markings, including the identification letters YKTN on the bow and stern, are a reflection of the US Navy's then current policy that carriers should be configured to allow aircraft operations in either direction. Just discernible abaft the island superstructure is the centre aircraft lift offset to starboard of the flight deck centreline. This arrangement required an extension of the port side of the flight deck to allow enough room for aircraft to move past the lift when it was in the lowered position.

Above: The aircraft on *Yorktown*'s deck in the previous photo are Grumman J2F utility amphibians. Later known officially as the Duck, the prototype XJF-1 flew in May 1933 and production JF-1s and JF-2s were supplied both to the Navy and the Marine Corps. The design incorporated several features of the Grumman FF-1 fighter but with an integral float married to the lower fuselage and into which the undercarriage retracted. The improved J2F was flown in April 1937 and several hundred were produced up to 1945. It was intended as a general-purpose utility aircraft and most carrier air groups included four or five such aircraft for ship-to-shore communication duties. This is a J2F-2A, an armed version of which nine were produced to equip Marine Squadron VMS-3 based in the Virgin Islands.

Opposite above: The second of the new 20,000-ton carriers was the USS *Enterprise* (CV-6), which was laid down on 16 July 1934, launched on 3 October 1936 and commissioned on 12 May 1938. In this photo she is lying in the James River off Newport News, VA, on 6 April 1938 after completing the builder's preliminary sea trials. For self-protection, the Yorktown class were to be armed with eight of the new 5-in/38 calibre dual-purpose guns distributed in single mountings sited quadrantally at the edges of the flight deck. They were also designed to carry four quadruple 1.1 machine-gun mountings but these were not available until sometime after the ships commissioned.

Opposite below: The USS *Enterprise* in late 1939, with aircraft belonging to Carrier Air Wing 6 (CVW-6) ranged on deck. At this time some of the new monoplane types were coming into service to replace the hitherto ubiquitous biplanes and an interesting mix of such types is illustrated here. Right aft are the Douglas TBD Devastators of VT-6 and in front of them are a few Northrop BT-1s of VB-6. Amidships are a few Grumman J2F amphibians and ahead of them a large group of Curtiss SBC Helldiver scout bombers. Finally, a few Grumman F3F-2 fighters belonging to VF-6 are ranged forward just behind the raised windbreak.

Above: The Douglas TBD-1 Devastator was the US Navy's first carrier-based monoplane to enter production, initially equipping VT-3 aboard the USS *Saratoga* in October 1937. With hook and undercarriage extended, one of that unit's aircraft is about to turn in towards the carrier for landing. Powered by a 900hp Pratt & Whitney R-1830 radial engine, the TBD had a cruising speed of 128mph and a range of 716 miles carrying a 1,000lb bomb or torpedo. It was the standard torpedo bomber aboard the carriers *Lexington*, *Saratoga*, *Yorktown* and *Enterprise* up to the opening stages of the Second World War but was withdrawn from operational use after suffering catastrophic losses at the Battle of Midway in May 1942.

Opposite above: A contemporary of the Douglas TBD and the second monoplane to equip carrier squadrons was the Vought SB2U Vindicator. Hedging its bets, the Navy initially ordered both monoplane and biplane (SB3U) versions of the new scout bomber but trials of both prototypes clearly established the superiority of the monoplane, which was ordered into production, the first examples reaching VB-3B (also aboard *Saratoga*) on 20 December 1937. It was powered by an 825hp Pratt & Whitney R-1535 radial engine and in the scout role had a range of 1,120 miles at a cruising speed of 152mph.

Opposite below: VB-3B proudly show off their new Vindicators in July 1938 with this formation of three aircraft posed against the backdrop of the Sierra Nevada mountains. Although the SB2U eventually equipped seven US Navy squadrons by the time the US entered the war in 1941, they had mostly been replaced and those remaining did not see any combat action. However, SBU-3s with composite Marine squadron VMSB-241 carried out attacks on the Japanese fleet at Midway in June 1941, but thereafter they were withdrawn from service. *NHIC*

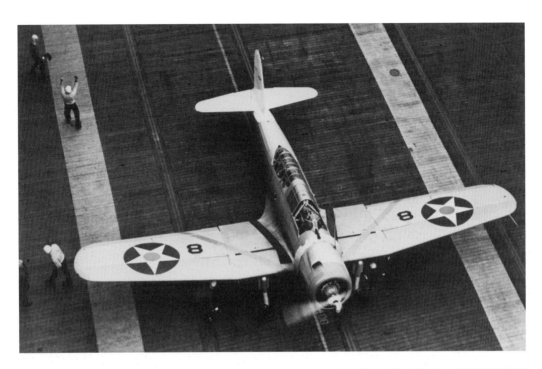

It wasn't only carrier-based naval aviation that progressed between the wars. The scout and observation aircraft carried by battleships and cruisers had important roles to play. These were invariably floatplanes which were launched by catapult and recovered by crane after alighting alongside. The most successful of these was the Curtiss SOC Seagull, which flew in prototype form in 1934 and production examples joined the fleet from November 1935 onwards. Over 300 were built and they remained in service until after the end of the Second World War. The four SOC-3 Seagulls in this formation are all from the section of Cruiser Scouting Squadron 9 (VCS-9) based aboard the light cruiser USS *Honolulu* (CL-48) in 1939. *NHIC*

As early as 1936, the Navy had selected a monoplane fighter designed by the Brewster Aeronautical Corporation and the prototype XF2A-1 shown here first flew in January 1938. In trials it outperformed the rival Grumman XF4F-2 and an initial contract for fifty-four F2A-1s was awarded. The first of these was delivered in late 1939, equipping VF-3 aboard the USS *Saratoga*, but in total, the US Navy only received eleven F2A-1s as the remainder were diverted to an order from Finland. Replacement F2A-2s with a more powerful engine and other changes did not reach Navy squadrons until September 1940.

Above: The original Grumman F4F was a biplane offering only incremental improvements over the F3F then in service. Consequently, the Navy revised the contract and the design was recast as the XF4F-2 monoplane, which flew in September 1937 and is illustrated here. Although slightly faster than the Brewster F2A, it was otherwise judged to be inferior and the prototype was returned to Grumman for further development. As rebuilt with a new wing, more powerful armament, revised tail surfaces and a 1,200hp supercharged R-1830 engine, it became the XF4F-3, which flew in March 1939 and demonstrated a substantially improved all-round performance. Consequently, the production F4F-3 quickly received substantial orders from Britain, France and Greece, as well as for the US Navy, which began operations with VF-41 in December 1940. *AC*

Opposite above: In the late 1920s the US Marine Corps began using Curtiss OC-1 Falcons as dive-bombers and their success led to a strong Navy interest in this form of attack. A developed version, the F8C-4 Helldiver, was produced for the Navy and entered service in 1930. This initiated a whole series of Curtiss dive-bombers that shared the Helldiver name, including the SBC, which entered service in 1937 and of which over 250 were produced. With a top speed of 237mph and capable of carrying a 1,000lb bomb, the SBC Helldiver was still in service at the time of Pearl Harbor in 1941, although mostly with reserve units such as this Oakland-based example. In fact, it was the last combat biplane to be produced for the US services (Army or Navy). *AC*

Opposite below: The USS *Lexington* (foreground) and USS *Saratoga* lying off Pearl Harbor following a series of fleet exercises in 1938. Earlier, during Fleet Problem XIX, on 29 March 1938 the two ships had launched a surprise dawn attack on Pearl Harbor which was assessed as very successful and even at that stage clearly showed the potential for such operations in wartime. Unfortunately, the lessons to be learnt from such examples were obviously not fully absorbed as the tragic events three years later were to show.

Chapter 4

Airships and Flying Boats

Alone among the world's major navies, it was only the US Navy that persevered with the development of lighter-than-air craft. After entering the war in 1917, the US Navy received a total of twenty-one non-rigid airships (universally known as Blimps) from its allies, and in the latter stages of the war and throughout the interwar period it developed a series of patrol blimps. However, under a 1921 agreement, the Army was responsible for land-based aircraft, so control and operation of the blimps was transferred to them. It was not until 1937 that the Navy regained control of the blimps, which proved to be a very useful asset in the following years. Ultimately, the Navy would acquire 241 blimps from 1917 until the last one was delivered in 1958, and airship operations did not finally cease until 1961.

Large rigid airships, with their long range and endurance, were ideally suited for missions over the ocean, and consequently the Navy retained responsibility for them. The US Navy ordered its first rigid airship (ZR-1 *Shenandoah*), which was built by the Naval Aircraft Factory and first flew in 1923. However, in order to speed up the airship programme, the incomplete British airship R38 was purchased and was ready for flight in 1921. Flown as the ZR-2, it was lost in a tragic accident in August of that year. Two German Zeppelins were awarded to the US as war reparations, but these were sabotaged prior to delivery and the Zeppelin company was ordered to build a replacement, which was delivered in 1924. Designated ZR-3, it was subsequently named as the USS *Los Angeles* and was destined to become the longest-serving US Navy rigid airship, only being scrapped in 1939.

The US Navy had still more ambitious plans for rigid airships and built two more (ZRS-4 USS *Akron* and ZRS-5 USS *Macon*), which flew in 1931 and 1933 respectively. These were two of the largest airships ever built, but the distinguishing feature was not their size but the purpose for which they were designed. In effect, they were flying aircraft carriers fitted with an internal hanger that could accommodate four high-performance biplane fighters. A retractable trapeze arrangement below the airship allowed aircraft to be launched and recovered while in flight. Unfortunately, both airships were lost in accidents in 1933 and 1935 respectively, and this was the end of the US Navy's rigid airship programme.

Apart from airships, the US Navy was also a world leader in the development of flying boats for maritime patrol purposes. With two long coastlines, and interests throughout the expanse of the Pacific, flying boats were an obvious choice for patrolling the seas. Following on from the PN series of flying boats produced in the 1920s, two major companies competed for Navy orders – the Consolidated Aircraft Corporation and the Glenn Martin Company. Between them, these two companies were responsible for supplying the Navy with most of the operational flying boats in the 1930s and throughout the Second World War.

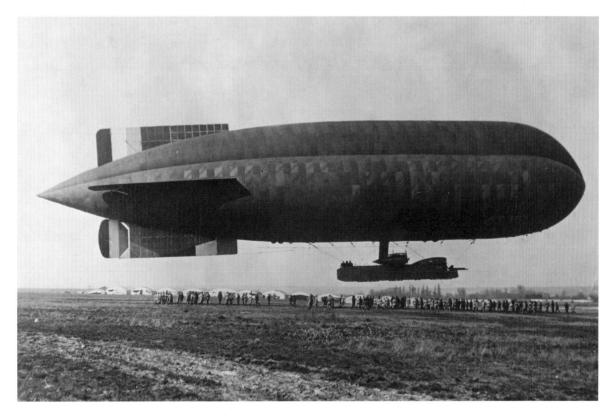

During the First World War, US Navy blimp operations in Europe relied substantially on craft supplied by Britain and France. The first coastal patrols were started in March 1918 using a French-built Astra-Torres non-rigid airship (AT-1) and later, sister ships AT-13 and AT-17. A fourth craft, AT-18 shown here, was ordered but completed records indicate that it was not handed over to the US Navy.

Above: In 1918 the US Navy ordered a semi-rigid airship from the Italian company Stabilimento Costruzioni Dirigibili ed Aerostati (SCDA). Designated O-1 and following successful flight tests, it was dismantled and shipped to the US and subsequently erected at Camp May airship base, New Jersey, where it flew on 16 September 1919. Powered by a pair of 125hp engines, it was actually the only semi-rigid airship to be operated by the US Navy, which instead favoured the less complex non-rigid blimps (a semi-rigid airship has a metal keel running the length of the gas envelope, helping to maintain shape and allowing heavier loads to be carried).

Opposite above: The first US Navy non-rigid airships to be produced in quantity were the B-Series and the first of sixteen examples (designated B-1 to B-16) was flown in May 1917. The rest were delivered over the next fifteen months. This is B-8, which was allocated the serial A242 and was built by Goodyear. The car below the airbag was basically a modified two-seater aeroplane fuselage and power was provided by a 100hp Curtiss OXX-2 engine driving a tractor propeller. From October 1917, most were employed on coastal patrols, mainly on the US East Coast, and flew over 13,500 hours on operational tasks. At the end of 1918, almost all were decommissioned and scrapped although two survived in the training role until 1924.

Opposite below: The ten C-Series blimps were a substantial improvement on the B-Series in that they were larger, were powered by two 150hp Wright Hispano engines and carried a crew of four. With a much greater endurance they were more suitable for coastal patrol and convoy protection tasks. However, the war ended before they could begin operational duties, and this is C-3 landing at Hampton Roads naval base in 1920. The C-Series were involved in several interesting projects including C-5, which flew the 1,400 miles from New York to Newfoundland on 14/15 May 1919 as the first stage of a projected transatlantic flight. Unfortunately, it was then lost when a gale tore it from its moorings.

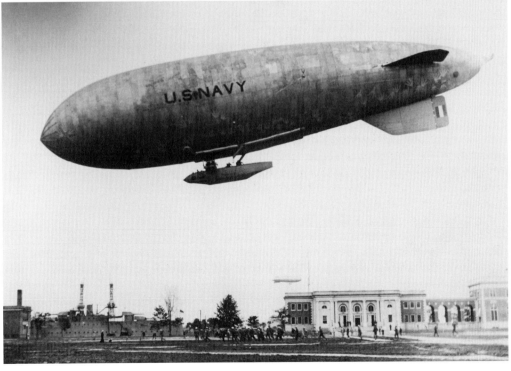

Above: The gondola of a C-Series airship showing the two Wright Hispano V-8 engines in open mountings with prominent radiators, each driving a pusher propeller. The two pipes hanging down from the airship's outer envelope are necessary to inflate the internal ballonets (air-filled bags that occupy the gaps between the gasbags as they expand or contract when the airship climbs or descends, and thus maintain the overall shape of the envelope) using the slipstream generated by the propellers. Just visible on the side of the gondola's rear section are a pair of bomb racks – a total of four 270lb bombs or depth charges could be carried.

Opposite above: Despite blimp operations being almost entirely delegated to the US Army between 1921 and 1937, the Navy continued to develop the concept through various prototypes. One of the most interesting was ZMC-2, which had a metal-clad envelope instead of the usual rubber and canvas material, and this was filled with helium. The enclosed gondola was attached directly to the gas envelope instead of being suspended below as in previous types. First flown in August 1929, the KMC-2 was powered by a pair of 220hp Wright J-5 Whirlwind air-cooled radial engines. Despite its unusual construction, this airship remained in service for ten years before being decommissioned in August 1939.

Opposite below: By the time that the United Sates became involved in the Second World War in 1941, the blimp had evolved into a sophisticated patrol craft capable of carrying out several functions not possible with conventional aircraft. The K-Series, which entered service in 1939, were a considerable advance on earlier types and at that time were the largest non-rigid airships ever built. The original K-1 flew in 1931 but was a one-off prototype. The larger K-2 shown here differed in many respects, including more powerful 550hp Pratt & Whiney Wasp radial engines, and was the first of 134 K-Series delivered before and during the Second World War. They were employed extensively on anti-submarine patrols over both the Atlantic and Pacific regions as well as in the Mediterranean theatre. Many remained in service in the post-war era and the last was not retired until 1959.

Above: ZR-1 was the designation allocated to the first US Navy rigid airship to be ordered, in August 1919. Its design was based on the German Zeppelin L.49 but construction was delayed due to a shortage of the newly developed Duralumin alloy required for the principal structures. Later it was decided, following experience with the ill-fated ZR-2, that the gas bags would be filled with helium instead of the highly inflammable hydrogen. Built by the Naval Aircraft Factory, it was assembled at NAS Lakehurst (New Jersey) and first flown on 4 August 1923, subsequently being commissioned as the USS *Shenandoah* (ZR-1) on 10 October 1923, and is shown here on an early test flight. *LoC*

Opposite above: As completed, the USS *Shenandoah* was powered by six 300hp Packard engines carried in separate gondolas, four arranged under the gas bag centre section, one on the centreline aft and one in the rear of the forward control gondola. The latter was removed in 1924 during repairs to damage caused when the ship was torn from its mooring mast during a gale in January 1924. She was back in service by May 1924 and is seen here over Bristol, Rhode Island, later that month. However, her brief career was ended on 3 September 1925 when the airship broke up in a storm over Southeast Ohio. Although fourteen crew were killed, another twenty-nine survived in some of the broken sections that floated down to the ground. Despite this tragic loss, the *Shenandoah* had shown the potential of airships during various fleet exercises.

The US Navy's first rigid airship to fly was actually ZR-2. This started life as the British R38, which had been ordered by the Admiralty in 1918, but when the project was cancelled after the end of the First World War the US Navy agreed to purchase the airship for the sum of $2 million. Completed in early summer 1921, it made its first test flight as ZR-2 on 23 June with a mixed US and British crew. On 23 August, it departed on what was intended as a long-range endurance test but while carrying out some manoeuvring tests it broke up and caught fire, all forty-eight occupants being killed in the resulting crash. This image, although of poor quality, is one of the few available showing ZR-2 in flight and its American markings can just be discerned. *LoC*

Above: One of the US Navy's more successful rigid airships, and the only one not to be lost in an accident, was the USS *Los Angeles* (ZR-3). Built by the Zeppelin company as the LZ-126 as part of Germany's war reparations, she first flew in August 1924. After testing, she left Friedrichshafen on 12 October to make a successful Atlantic crossing and arrived at Lakehurst three days later, after just over eighty-two hours in the air. Over the next few years she made several long-distance flights and was mainly involved in training crews and trialling new equipment for the forthcoming new airships ZR-4 and ZR-5. The photo shows USS *Los Angeles* in 1926 over Washington DC, with the famous Union Station visible under the tail section.

Opposite above: The USS *Los Angeles* (ZR-3) moored to USS *Patoka* (AO-9), which was converted from an oiler in 1924 to act as a support ship for the new airships. The top of the mooring mast stood 141 feet above the waterline, allowing the airship to swing in any direction but remain above the parent ship. Noticeable in this view is that the crew gondola is attached directly to the bottom of the hull envelope rather than suspended below as in the earlier airships. *Los Angeles* remained operational for eight years and in 1931 and 1932 took part in major fleet exercises before being laid up in June 1932. By the time she decommissioned, she had flown for 4,398 hours during some 331 flights, which equates to average flight times in excess of thirteen hours – illustrating the long endurance flights of which airships were capable.

The USS *Akron* (ZRS-4) was the first of two massive aircraft carrying airships ordered by the US Navy in 1928. She was built at Akron, Ohio, by the Goodyear-Zeppelin Corporation and made her first flight on 23 September 1931. After successful flight trials she was formally commissioned amid great ceremony on 27 October 1931 at the Navy airship base at Lakehurst, New Jersey. This photo shows *Akron* approaching Camp Kearney, CA, on 11 May 1932 after a transcontinental flight from the East Coast. Shortly afterwards, a combination of circumstances caused the airship to rise uncontrollably with four sailors still holding onto the mooring ropes. One let go quickly and was injured but two others rose higher and subsequently fell to their deaths. The fourth sailor, Apprentice Seaman 'Bud' Cowart, tied himself to the line and was eventually hauled aboard the airship, which then succeeded in landing safely.

Above: The aircraft intended to operate from the airships *Akron* and *Macon* was the Curtiss F9C-2 Sparrowhawk. The original XF9C-1 was designed as a small fighter for conventional aircraft carrier operations and first flew on 12 February 1931. After competitive trials, and following some modifications, six production F9C-2 Sparrowhawks were delivered in the summer of 1932. These featured Wright R-975 engines, a repositioned top wing to improve pilot view and, most noticeably, a sturdy skyhook structure that enabled the aircraft to latch onto a trapeze suspended below the airships.

Opposite above: Initial trials with a trapeze mechanism had been carried out in 1931 using a temporary installation under the USS *Los Angeles* (ZR-3), which, of course, had no hanger facility. This view shows Lieutenant Howard L. Young USN piloting the original XF9C-1 on the first hook-up to the USS *Akron* on 3 May 1932. Once secured to the trapeze, the aircraft was hoisted up to the hangar deck, where it was transferred to an overhead gantry system that would move it to one of the hanger corners, where up to four aircraft could be stowed.

Opposite below: *Akron* was powered by eight 560hp Maybach V-12 petrol engines mounted inside the hull to reduce drag and driving the two-bladed propellers via extension shafts and gears. The propeller hubs were capable of being rotated to provide thrust from the horizontal through to the vertical planes, which greatly aided manoeuvrability. This photo was taken on 4 March 1933 as *Akron* overflew New York and Manhattan. Almost exactly a month later, on the night of 3/4 April, she had departed from Lakehurst on a routine flight off the New England coast when she encountered severe weather conditions, including violent gusts and downdrafts. The tail struck the water and the tail fin was torn off, making the ship uncontrollable. It sank onto the sea and rapidly broke up. There were only three survivors out of the seventy-six people on board and one of the casualties was Rear Admiral William A. Moffett, who had been the major driving force behind the airship aircraft carrier concept.

Above: The second aircraft-carrying airship was the USS *Macon* (ZRS-5), whose construction was begun at Goodyear's Akron plant in May 1931. Its first flight occurred on 21 April 1933, just over two weeks after the tragic loss of the *Akron*. In this view of the underside, the opening for the aircraft hanger is clearly visible with a Consolidated N2Y trainer ready to be lowered and flown off. The N2Y, an adapted two-seat trainer, was used as a 'ship's boat' to convey passengers and spare parts between the airship and ground airfields. The vertical panels on the side of the envelope above each of the propeller transmissions housed condensers that extracted water from the engine exhausts to replenish ballast water used in manoeuvring.

Opposite above: An F9C-2 Sparrowhawk about to engage on the USS *Macon's* lowered trapeze. Once hooked on, steadying arms on either side of the trapeze would be lowered and attached to strongpoints on the upper surface of the wings. Once this was done, the rear yoke would be lowered over the rear fuselage and the firmly attached aircraft could then be raised into the hanger. The pilot would keep the engine running until actually level with the hanger deck in case it became necessary to release the aircraft due to a malfunction or emergency. The Sparrowhawks proved reliable in service and once aboard the airship, the undercarriage was often removed (not needed for trapeze operations) and replaced by a 30-gallon (US) fuel tank.

Opposite below: The USS *Macon* pictured over NAS Moffet (California) in March 1934. *Macon* first arrived there on 15 October 1933 and it was to be her base for the next sixteen months apart from a detachment in April/May 1934 for exercises in the Caribbean. While en route to Florida she suffered structural damage when part of one of her rear frames (17.5) collapsed and only quick action by the repair crew saved the ship. Once back at Moffet, the airship was involved in a series of exercises with the fleet and began to show its true potential as a significant scouting asset, a process enhanced by the extended 255-mile operating radius of the F9C Sparrowhawks with their external fuel tanks.

Some idea of the sheer size of the USS *Macon* can be gauged as it emerges from the specially built Hanger One at NAS Moffet, which was completed in 1933. However, its role as a base for the USS *Macon* was short-lived as the airship was tragically lost on the night of 12 February 1935 when storm gusts caused the partially repaired frame 17.5 to fail again, this time rupturing the adjacent gas bags. Potentially the ship could have been saved but the bridge crew, unaware of the exact nature and location of the damage, released too much ballast. With engines still running at full power, the ship rose rapidly in an extreme tail down attitude to an altitude of over 4,000 feet. This caused the pressure valves to lift and a massive amount of helium was lost, which, coupled with the loss of the two rear gas bags, made the airship uncontrollable and it drifted down rapidly into the sea. Fortunately, of the eighty-three men on board, almost all were rescued and there were only two fatalities.

Another important aspect of naval aviation were the numerous patrol wings equipped with long-range flying boats mainly produced by the Consolidated and Martin companies. The Navy's first monoplane flying boat was the Consolidated XPY-1, which was built to a Naval Aircraft Factory specification and first flew in 1929. However, under the naval tendering scheme, the contract for a developed version went to Martin, who produced it in small numbers as the Martin P3M-1. A later version was the P3M-2 shown here, which featured an enclosed crew cockpit and more powerful Pratt & Whitney Hornet engines, but only half a dozen were built and the P3M only served briefly with VP-10S in 1931–32 before being withdrawn for training and other duties. *NHIC*

Despite initially losing out to Martin, Consolidated continued to develop their XPY-1 design and produced the P2Y-1, which was similar but incorporated a small lower wing in a sesquiplane configuration. Twenty-three were ordered and all but two were modified to P2Y-2 configuration in which the engines, instead of being mounted between the wing, were positioned in nacelles attached to the upper wing leading edge. This reduced drag and substantially boosted performance. A further twenty-three were built to the same configuration as the P2Y-3. The P2Y-1 entered service in 1933, followed by the new-build P2Y-3 in 1935. They served with six patrol squadrons for several years but by late 1941, most were based at Pensacola as trainers.

On 28 March 1935, Consolidated flew their prototype XP3Y, which was the forerunner of one of the most famous flying boats ever produced. It was to be better known as the Catalina, although that name was not officially adopted by the US Navy until late 1941. To demonstrate the aircraft's potential, on 14–15 October 1935, it was flown from Coco Solo (Panama) to NAS Almeda (California) in 34 hours 45 minutes, covering a distance of 3,443 miles, which was a world record for seaplanes. The crew, commanded by Lieutenant Commander Knefler McGinnis, pose alongside the prototype after their epic flight. The fact that the XP3Y could carry a 4,000lb bomb load or two torpedoes led to it being redesignated as a patrol bomber (PBY). Improved versions were ordered in quantity and by the time of Pearl Harbor in 1941, it equipped virtually all of the US Navy's Patrol Wings in both the Pacific and Atlantic fleets.

Chapter 5

Going to War

At the opening of a new decade in 1940, Europe was already at war. Despite a strong domestic sentiment of non-American involvement, President Roosevelt astutely steered legislation through Congress that allowed large-scale expansion of the Army and Navy. The new carrier USS *Wasp* joined the fleet in April 1940 and was followed by the USS *Hornet* in October 1941. In the meantime, a new class of carriers was being developed and, free from any treaty restrictions, displacement rose to 27,000 tons, which allowed for much improved aviation facilities. These were the Essex class, and although the first was laid down in April 1941, it was not until mid-1943 that they became available for operations.

As far as aircraft were concerned, the trend to monoplanes continued. The improved Grumman F4F-3 Wildcat began to reach fleet units at the end of 1940, and by late 1941 was the standard fighter aboard all the US Navy carriers. It completely supplanted the Brewster Buffalo, which lingered on until mid-1942 with a number of USMC squadrons. The other important addition was the Douglas SBD Dauntless dive-bomber, which entered service with Marine Corps squadrons at the end of 1940 and by the end of 1941 had equipped seven Navy squadrons based aboard the carriers, where they replaced Curtis SBC Helldiver biplanes. The SBD proved to be a tough and enduring aircraft, much liked by its crews, and it would remain in front-line service almost until the end of the war.

At dawn on 7 December 1941, the Japanese launched the now infamous attack on Pearl Harbor. In the ensuing carnage, most of the Pacific Fleet's battleships were sunk or seriously damaged and dozens of naval aircraft were destroyed on the ground. Fortunately, the aircraft carriers were not present as *Lexington* and *Enterprise* were engaged on missions to ferry aircraft to Midway and Wake islands respectively, while *Saratoga* was at San Diego having just completed a refit. *Yorktown* was stationed on the east coast with the Atlantic Fleet, but a few days later was transferred to the Pacific Fleet. The brand-new carrier *Hornet* had just joined the fleet and was still working up, but once fully operational she was assigned the lead role in the spectacular Doolittle Raid on Japan itself.

In strategic terms the Doolittle Raid achieved very little and a more alarming development was the southward incursion of Japanese forces intent on occupying New Guinea and threatening the vital communication routes between the US and

Australia. The carriers *Lexington* and *Yorktown* were deployed as the core of a task force sent to stop the enemy advance; the outcome was the Battle of the Coral Sea, which occurred on 7/8 May 1942. This has significance as the first naval battle fought entirely between the air fleets of the carriers involved and in which the ships of either side were never in visual contact with each other; it clearly illustrated that the day of the battleship as the prime element in naval warfare had passed.

There was to be little respite for the US Navy as, a month later, Admiral Yamamoto launched Operation MI, which involved almost the entire Japanese Combined Fleet. The nominal objective was the capture of the US-held Midway Island, but this was intended to bring about a major engagement in which the US Pacific Fleet would be annihilated. However, Admiral Nimitz (C-in-C Pacific) had advance warning due to Navy codebreakers being able to read some of the enemy messages and was able to deploy his three available carriers in a position to meet the threat. The epic battle that followed was an emphatic victory for the US Navy and brought a stop to Japan's up to then almost unchecked advance across the Pacific. There were still hard battles to be fought, but the tide was turning.

On 25 April 1940, the US Navy commissioned its latest aircraft carrier – the USS *Wasp* (CV-7). When she was laid down in April 1936 the tonnage limitations of the Washington Treaty still applied and only 15,000 tons was available for the new carrier. Consequently, although based on the *Yorktown*, there were several significant modifications in order to reduce displacement. The shorter hull resulted in a reduction of 80 feet on the length of the flight deck, less powerful two-shaft machinery reduced speed to less than 30 knots, and there was no specific anti-torpedo protection. Nor could she embark a torpedo bomber squadron as there was no provision for torpedo stowage.

Opposite above: USS *Yorktown* (CV-5) at North Island embarking aircraft before sailing to Hawaii in June 1940. As well as her own air group, the crowded flight deck also carries many other aircraft destined to be offloaded ashore at Hawaii and this provides an interesting snapshot of US Naval aviation at that time. Biplanes include F3F fighters and SBC Helldivers, while the new monoplanes are represented by SB2U Vindicators and a few Northrop BT-1s. Ranged amidships are six Sikorsky JRS flying boats with their outer wings removed, as well as a couple of Grumman JRF amphibians.

Opposite below: The last carrier to enter service before the US became involved in the war was the USS *Hornet* (CV-8). Freed from treaty restrictions, the US Navy was able to lay down a new 20,000-ton Yorktown class in September 1939 and *Hornet* subsequently commissioned on 20 October 1941, only six weeks before Pearl Harbor. This photo was taken in mid-1941 while carrying out contractor's trails prior to commissioning, and at that stage her armament of eight single 5-in guns and four quadruple 1.1 machine-gun mountings had not been fitted. *NHIC*

In December 1940, the US Navy began to receive deliveries of the Grumman F4F Wildcat, which was destined to become the Navy's only carrier-based operational fighter until well into 1943. The initial production version was the F4F-3, which did not have folding wings but by the end of 1941, when the US was at war, a total of 248 Wildcats (the name officially adopted at that time) were on strength, including these examples of VF-3 aboard USS *Saratoga*. Although the previous colourful squadron markings have been discarded in favour of an overall grey camouflage, full squadron identification codes are carried. *NHIC*

Above: The widespread introduction of the F4F Wildcat rapidly relegated the rival Brewster F2A Buffalo, which had briefly equipped VF-2 and VF-3 aboard *Lexington* and *Saratoga*, to second-line training duties, as illustrated by this F2A-2 pictured in August 1942. The only examples to see combat action were those of Marine Squadron VMF-221 at Midway in June 1942, where they were severely outclassed by the Japanese Mitsubishi A6M (Zero) fighters.

Opposite above: The US Navy's main base in the Pacific was Pearl Harbor at Oahu in the Hawaiian Islands in mid-1941. At top right is Ford Island, the main naval airfield in the area, in front of which can be seen several battleships on their row of moorings, and just discernible at the top end is the dark grey shape of a carrier (probably USS *Lexington*). In the centre is the naval dockyard with rows of oil storage tanks in the foreground. On the left edge of the picture can be seen the hangers and landing strip of Hickam Field, the main USAAC airfield. All in all, a very tempting range of targets!

Opposite below: Just before 0800 hrs on 7 December 1941, Japanese carrier-based aircraft mounted a surprise attack on Pearl Harbor. Despite the tense political situation at the time, as well as the demonstrated potential of air attacks in various fleet exercises, the defences at Pearl Harbor were literally caught with their pants down! This dramatic image was taken from one of the Japanese aircraft shortly after the attack commenced and in the water can be seen the tracks of the two torpedoes that hit the battleship USS *West Virginia* (BB-48), together with the outward ripples of the resulting explosions. In the background, smoke rises from Hickam Field, which was also under attack.

Fortunately, the Pacific Fleet carriers were not present at Pearl Harbor when it was attacked. Nevertheless, Japanese attacks on the naval air stations at Ford Island and Kaneohe (on the east coast of Oahu), as well as the Marine Air Corps station at Ewa, took a heavy toll of the neatly parked aircraft. Out of about 250 Navy and Marine aircraft on Oahu, only fifty-four were left at the end of the day. At Kaneohe, where thirty-six PBY Catalinas were based, twenty-seven were destroyed and six damaged; the other three only escaped because they were airborne on patrol at the time. This photo gives some idea of the destruction wrought, with a Grumman JRF Duck in the foreground completely destroyed and smoke from burning Catalinas forming a backdrop. *NHIC*

Wake Island, which lies roughly halfway between Hawaii and the Philippines, was attacked by Japanese forces on 8 December 1941, and despite heroic resistance by the US forces, it finally fell on 23 December. In the aftermath of Pearl Harbor, offensive action by the US Pacific Fleet was limited to hit-and-run carrier strikes against Japanese-held islands. On 24 February 1942, TF.8 centred on the carrier USS *Enterprise* and commanded by Vice-Admiral Halsey, mounted a bombing raid against Wake Island; these SBD-3 Dauntless of VB-6 are preparing for take-off from the *Enterprise*. On 4 March, these aircraft made a follow-up strike against Marcus Island, lying further to the west.

Above: A Douglas TBD-1 of VT-6 from *Enterprise* overflies Wake Island while the raid is in progress and smoke drifting from targets already hit is visible below. This aircraft is finished in a camouflage scheme introduced progressively from mid-1941 and consists of light grey undersides and a grey/green finish on the upper services. The national markings still include a red dot in the centre of the white star, and red and white striped tail surfaces.

Opposite above: The raids on Wake Island and other targets did little to impress the Japanese but gave valuable combat experience to the US aircrews. However, another raid launched on 16 April 1942 was to have an effect out of all proportion to the limited material damage it would cause. This was the famous Tokyo (or Doolittle) Raid in which sixteen USAAF B-25 Mitchell bombers, led by Lieutenant Colonel James Doolittle, were launched from the USS *Hornet* (CV-8). The bombers were stowed on deck and most of her normal air group were stowed below in the hanger. Here, the carrier is escorted by the destroyer USS *Gwin* (DD433) and the light cruiser USS *Nashville* (CL-43).

Opposite below: On 13 April 1942, *Hornet* and her escorts met with *Enterprise* and her group, the two forces combining to become TF.16 under Halsey. Apart from the two carriers, there were four cruisers and eight destroyers, and while *Hornet*'s deck was blocked by the B-25s, the air defence of the force was entrusted to the F4F Wildcats of VF-6 aboard the *Enterprise*. This shows *Hornet* underway at that time with the B-25s ranged on deck and the heavy cruiser USS *Vincennes* (CA-44) in the background.

Above: It was intended that the B-25s would be launched approximately 450 miles from Tokyo but the task force was sighted by Japanese picket boats when still 700 miles away. In order to retain an element of surprise it was decided to launch the bombers at that point. The take-offs were heart-stopping moments for all concerned and the first bomber away, flown by Doolittle himself, was the most critical as it had the shortest take-off run. Following aircraft had progressively more flight deck as the others took off ahead. However, all sixteen of the bombers got airborne safely and set course for their targets.

Opposite above: The original plan was that the bombers would reach Tokyo and other targets during the night and then fly on to Chinese airfields, where they would arrive after dawn. The unscheduled early take-off meant that they reached their targets in daylight but then were over the Chinese mainland in darkness and, unable to find the airfields, the crews bailed out or made forced landings as they ran short of fuel. Although material damage was slight, the sight of US bombers over Japan forced the Japanese to invest precious resources to the defence of the homeland, while the morale effect for the American people was tremendous. This is a view from one of the B-25s over Yokosuka naval base, and a Japanese destroyer and auxiliary are just visible at the bottom edge of the photo.

Opposite below: While *Enterprise* and *Hornet* were completing their mission in the Central Pacific, US naval intelligence became aware of Japanese plans to capture Port Moresby on the south side of New Guinea and also to set up a seaplane base on the island of Tulagi in the lower Solomon Islands. If successful, these moves would effectively cut seaborne communications between the US and Australia. Accordingly, the carriers *Yorktown* and *Lexington*, as TF.17 under Rear Admiral Fletcher, were dispatched to the Coral Sea with orders stop the Japanese advance. For three days, the opposing fleets played blind man's bluff in difficult weather conditions but on 7 May, US planes located the light carrier *Shōhō* and promptly sank her, causing the Japanese to abandon their invasion attempt. This view shows the carrier under attack only minutes before she sank.

Early the following day, the main enemy force was located and the Japanese carrier *Shōkaku* was severely damaged by aircraft from the US carriers, although they were unable to locate the carrier *Zuikaku*, which was masked by a rain squall. However, at almost the same time (1110 hrs), Japanese aircraft attacked the *Lexington*, which was hit by at least two torpedoes and two bombs, causing some damage and starting fires. Nevertheless, about an hour later, *Lexington*'s crew had succeeded in extinguishing the fires and reduced an initial 7° list by transferring fuel oil, and were beginning to pump out three flooded boiler rooms. At this stage, the ship was able to recommence flight deck operations, and here a TBD Devastator has just landed on, with an F4F Wildcat on approach astern.

Unfortunately, at 1247 hrs, the ship was racked by a violent explosion caused by fumes from leaking fuel, which started several new fires and triggered more explosions. Even at this point the ship could still make 25 knots and a few aircraft were able to land on before the smoke got too dense, but by 1515 hrs, all flight operations had ceased and wounded sailors and unnecessary personnel including aircrew were starting to be evacuated from the ship. The destroyer *Morris* (DD417) had come alongside to assist in fighting the fires, but rising temperatures in the engine rooms caused them to be abandoned and *Lexington* drifted to standstill at 1630 hrs. Other destroyers were then able to close and pick up survivors. Here, *Morris* is still alongside abreast the funnel and USS *Hammann* (DD412) is closing astern. *NARA*

Above: At 1830 hrs, the warheads in the torpedo store amidships cooked off, causing an enormous explosion that effectively spelt the end of the ship and she was finished off by torpedoes from a destroyer. Despite the horrendous events of the day, a total of 2,735 officers and men had been saved – virtually the entire crew apart from 216 who had been killed in the attacks or resulting explosions. The Battle of the Coral Sea was the first to be fought entirely by carrier-based aircraft and resulted in the loss of the USS *Lexington* and damage to the USS *Yorktown*. The Japanese lost the small carrier *Shōhō* (12,000 tons) while the larger *Shōkaku* was seriously damaged and was lucky to make it back to Japan. Despite the sad loss of the *'Lady Lex'*, the attack on Port Moresby was abandoned and *Yorktown* was repaired in time to play a vital role at the Battle of Midway only four weeks later, so the overall outcome was ultimately more favourable to the US Navy.

Opposite above: Even while the Battle of the Coral Sea was being fought, Admiral Nimitz was aware of a more ambitious Japanese plan in which the nominal objective was to occupy the Aleutians and Midway Island. However, Admiral Yamamoto saw this as a means of drawing out the remaining assets of the US Pacific Fleet, which would then be annihilated by the superior Japanese Combined Fleet, which totalled no fewer than 162 ships, including seven aircraft carriers. To oppose them, Nimitz had only seventy-four ships, of which a third were too far away in the North Pacific to participate in the crucial action off Midway. His main strength lay in the three available carriers, *Enterprise*, *Hornet* and *Yorktown*. The first two, shown here, formed the basis of TF.16 commanded by Rear Admiral Raymond Spruance, while TF.17 under Rear Admiral Fletcher was built around the *Yorktown*, which had been hastily repaired at Pearl Harbor following damage incurred in the Coral Sea battle. The two forces met up on 2 June 1942 – only just in time.

Opposite below: On 4 June, the Japanese carriers launched an attack against Midway while a variety US aircraft based on the island took off to seek out the enemy carriers. Here, the carrier *Hiryū* successfully manoeuvres to avoid sticks of bombs dropped from high altitude by four USAAF B-17s based on Midway. Other attacks mounted by USAAF B-26 Marauders and Navy TBF Avengers were equally unsuccessful and seventeen US aircraft were shot down, including five out of the six Avengers.

Unbeknown to Nagumo, the three US carriers under the tactical command of Rear Admiral Raymond Spruance were only 200 miles away to the north-east. Although scout planes from Japanese cruisers had been tasked to search in that sector, two of them were delayed due to technical problems and did not locate the US carriers until Nagumo had committed his squadrons to a second strike on Midway. By that time, Spruance had already ordered a strike force to be launched at maximum range. This is the scene aboard the *Enterprise* as she prepared to launch the Douglas TBD torpedo bombers of VT-6. Sadly, it must be recorded that subsequently, ten of the fourteen TBDs were shot down in abortive attacks on the Japanese carriers. Also, VT-3 from *Yorktown* lost eight out of twelve, while *Hornet*'s entire VT-8 squadron (fifteen aircraft) was completely wiped out – all for no effect.

A Douglas TBD-1 Devastator belonging to VT-6, the torpedo bomber squadron forming part of *Enterprise*'s air group. This photo was taken as the aircraft flew over Hawaii in April 1942. A few weeks later, this aircraft was in action at Midway but was shot down while attempting to attack the Japanese carrier *Kaga*. Both the pilot, Lieutenant Paul James Riley, and his gunner, Edwin John Mushinski, were killed. So many TBDs were lost at Midway that the type was withdrawn from front-line service after the battle; its replacement in the torpedo bomber role was the Grumman TBF/TBM Avenger, then just beginning to enter service. *NHIC*

Above: Hornet's air group prepares to take off on the morning of 4 June for strikes against the Japanese carriers. In the foreground are the F4F-4s of VF-8 and ranged behind are the SBDs of VS-8. The Wildcats are of interest in that *Hornet* was the first carrier to receive the F4F-4 version, which had a heavier armament (six 0.5in machine guns) but, more importantly, was the first to feature folding wings. Unfortunately, the aircraft seen here were to have little success. Due to a navigation error, the formations (apart from VT-8) failed to find the Japanese fleet and all ten Wildcats had to ditch after running out of fuel, although most of the dive-bombers eventually made it back to the carrier. *NHIC*

Opposite above: Despite the calamitous losses among the torpedo bomber squadrons, they at least had the effect of drawing down the defending Zero fighters and occupying the attention of the AA gunners. Consequently, the arrival overhead of almost fifty SBD dive-bombers from *Enterprise* (VB-6 and VS-6) and *Yorktown* (VB-3 and VS-5) went unnoticed until it was too late. Within minutes, the carriers *Akagi, Kaga* and *Sōryū* were blazing wrecks as direct hits ignited secondary explosions among the fully armed aircraft ranged on deck. Losses amongst the SBDs were not as bad as those experienced by the torpedo bombers although even so, over a dozen were shot down. One survivor was this damaged SBD-3 from *Enterprise's* VB-6, which, short of fuel, landed on the USS *Yorktown* after successfully attacking the Japanese carrier *Kaga. NHIC*

The security offered by *Yorktown* was short-lived as around midday she was attacked by Val dive-bombers from the remaining Japanese carrier, *Hiryū*. Hit by three bombs, she drifted to a standstill, but her damage-control teams managed to get her underway again and the flight deck was shored up to allow flight operations to continue. However, two hours later, *Hiryū*'s Kate torpedo bombers made another attack, scoring two hits which resulted in the ship listing heavily to port (see photo). Fearing that the ship would sink, Captain Buckmaster ordered the crew to abandon ship although later that evening she was still afloat and volunteer crew went back on board to prepare for a tow to Pearl Harbor. All this was in vain as she was again torpedoed, on this occasion by the Japanese submarine I-168, on 5 June, and she eventually sank later the following day.

Revenge was quickly taken. In the late afternoon, a scout plane from *Yorktown* found the remaining Japanese carrier, *Hiryū*, and Spruance immediately ordered all available aircraft to be launched for a strike. Eventually, twenty-four SBDs were mustered from VB-6 and VS-6 aboard the *Enterprise*, together with another fourteen from VB-3 (originally part of *Yorktown*'s air group but now operating from *Enterprise*). Despite being intercepted by Zero fighters, the strike force pressed home their attack and scored four or five hits on the Japanese carrier, which was then completely disabled. However, the *Hiryū* stayed afloat for several hours before finally going down the following morning. *NHIC*

Chapter 6

Atlantic and Europe

Prior to Pearl Harbor, the carriers *Yorktown*, *Wasp* and *Ranger* were allocated to the Atlantic Fleet, and although *Yorktown* was then transferred to the Pacific, *Wasp* and *Ranger* became intimately involved in the war against Germany. In March 1942, *Wasp* sailed as part of a task force dispatched at Churchill's request to reinforce the British Home Fleet based at Scapa Flow. Subsequently, the carrier, escorted by Royal Navy warships, was sent in May to the Mediterranean on a mission to fly off desperately needed Spitfires to reinforce Malta's defences. Later she was recalled for deployment to the Pacific, where she was sorely needed.

On the other hand, the USS *Ranger* operated in the Atlantic theatre for most of the war. Even before Pearl Harbor, she acted as escort for a British troop convoy and in November 1942 she was at the centre of the task force covering the US landings during Operation Torch, the Allied invasion of North Africa. Later she operated with the British Home Fleet and in September 1943, her aircraft carried out a successful strike against German shipping in the Norwegian port of Bodø. There was little carrier-based US naval aviation involvement in the invasion of Sicily and the subsequent landings at Salerno and Anzio. Even for Operation Overlord, the D-Day Normandy landings on 6 June 1944, US Navy observation squadrons normally based aboard the battleships and cruisers were landed and their supporting missions flown from shore bases using borrowed Spitfires. However, the follow-up Operation Dragoon, the invasion of the south of France, involved considerable carrier-based air support, which was provided by a mixed task force of British and US escort carriers.

The concept of an escort carrier had arisen even before the war but the depredations of the German U-boats hastened their development and construction. The first US-built escort carrier was the USS *New York* (AVG-1), which commissioned in 1941 and set the pattern for the construction of no fewer than 124 similar vessels, many of which were transferred to the Royal Navy. Early escort carriers were based on or adapted from mercantile hulls before production lines were set to produce a standardised design. Although less glamorous than the various fleet actions, the Battle of the Atlantic was probably the most important and certainly the most drawn-out campaign of the war. If the U-boat had not been defeated then the various invasions, including Overlord in 1944, could not have happened. As more escort carriers became available they were allocated to hunter-killer anti-submarine groups, some of which were very successful.

One issue that urgently needed addressing was the provision of maritime patrol aircraft. Under an agreement dating back to 1920, the Army would be responsible for all combat aircraft that operated from land bases. Consequently, when the US entered the war in December 1941 and U-boats began operating off the US east coast, the Navy had no land-based maritime patrol aircraft. Belatedly, in October 1942 the Anti-submarine Army Command was formed, but this was not satisfactory as the Army aircrews lacked the training and experience for operations over the sea, and it was disbanded in August 1943 when responsibility for anti-submarine operations passed entirely to the US Navy. At least some long-range B-24 Liberators were made available and put into service as the PB4Y, but it wasn't until well into 1943 that they were available in reasonable numbers. The other significant land-based patrol aircraft was the Lockheed PV Ventura, which had been developed from the Hudson that was supplied to the British RAF from 1939. During all this time, the backbone of the anti-submarine effort remained the proven PBY Catalina flying boats that equipped numerous Fleet Air Wings. Later they were supplemented by the larger and more capable Martin PBM Mariner.

Opposite: In late March 1942, at Churchill's request, the US Navy dispatched Task Force 39 across the Atlantic to reinforce the Royal Navy's Home Fleet at Scapa Flow. This consisted of a modern battleship (USS *Washington* BB-56), two heavy cruisers and eight destroyers, but the most important asset was the carrier USS *Wasp* (CV-7). She is shown here viewed from the Royal Navy cruiser HMS *Edinburgh*, which met the US ships in as they approached British waters on 3 April. Ranged on deck are F4F Wildcat fighters of VF-71 and SB2U Vindicator torpedo bombers of VS-71 or VS-72.

Due to the sensitivity of US relations with Vichy France, Churchill had initially assured Roosevelt that the US ships would not be deployed to Gibraltar or the Mediterranean. However, by the time they arrived at Scapa Flow the situation at Malta had become critical and permission was given for *Wasp* to participate in Operation Calendar, an attempt to fly in Spitfires to bolster the island's defences. The carrier left Scapa and proceeded to Glasgow, where she embarked a total of forty-seven Spitfire Mk.Vc fighters. These were hoisted aboard by crane, with wingtips removed to facilitate stowage in the ship's hanger. Subsequently, they were flown off on 20 April 1942, but no sooner had they landed on Malta than the Luftwaffe launched a strong attack and all but a few were destroyed or damaged on the ground.

Above: The loss of most of the first batch of Spitfires at Malta made a second mission essential. This was Operation Bowery, in which *Wasp* was accompanied by the RN carrier HMS *Eagle*, which carried seventeen additional Spitfires. Here, the British carrier can be seen behind Spitfires and a Wildcat ranged on *Wasp*'s after flight deck. Including *Eagle*'s contribution, a total of sixty-one Spitfires safely reached Malta on 9 May, where, having learnt the lessons of the previous debacle, efficient arrangements were in place to protect the fighters while they were quickly rearmed and refuelled in time to meet the subsequent enemy air raids. The successful establishment of Spitfire squadrons on Malta represented a significant turning point in the island's fortunes.

Opposite above: USS *Wasp* was back at Scapa Flow by 15 May, where she is anchored with the British carrier HMS *Victorious* just beyond. In the background are the battleships HMS *King George V* (at left) and USS *Washington* (centre). Also visible (centre right) is the cruiser USS *Wichita* (CA-45). The US ships were now redesignated as Task Force 99 but when they detached to Hvalfjordur in Iceland on 20 May, the *Wasp* continued westwards to Norfolk, VA, for a short refit. Thereafter she proceeded to the Pacific, where she was sorely needed after the loss of *Lexington* and *Yorktown*.

Opposite below: The USS *Ranger* was the least successful of the pre-war US carriers. Smaller than the later Yorktown class, her slim hull resulted in an uneasy motion in anything but fair conditions and this often curtailed flight operations. When Churchill requested that *Ranger* be sent to the Indian Ocean to bolster the Eastern Fleet, Roosevelt demurred on the grounds that the US Navy 'was not proud of her compartmentation and structural strength', although this was said partly to avoid putting the ship under Royal Navy command. In any event, she was deemed unsuitable for service with the Pacific Fleet and spent most of the war in Atlantic waters.

In early November 1941, *Ranger* was deployed as part of the escort for a large convoy (WS-12X) sailing from Halifax to India and made up of US troopships. Despite the fact that America was not yet at war and the convoy and its escort consisted entirely of US ships, the troops carried (almost 20,000 men) were soldiers of the British 18th Infantry Division – an outstanding but relatively unpublicised example of the assistance accorded to Britain under Roosevelt's 'short of war' policy. Here, one of *Ranger's* SB2U scout bombers flies over the convoy, where the leading row of ships (from left to right) consists of the troopships *West Point* (AP-23), *Vernon* (AP-22) and *Wakefield* (AP-21), as well as one of the escorting cruisers, USS *Quincy* (CA-39).

Vought SB2U-1 Vindicators belonging to VS-41 and VS-42 aboard USS *Ranger* in November 1941 warm up in preparation for anti-submarine patrols. Each is armed with a single 325lb Mk.XVII depth charge. Just visible at right is the tail of an F4F-3 Wildcat of VF-41; in December 1940, *Ranger* had been the first US carrier to receive the new monoplane fighter.

After completing two ferry trips across the Atlantic carrying USAAF P-40 fighters, *Ranger* was allocated to Task Force 34 assembling for Operation Torch, the Allied landings in North Africa, which began on 8 November 1942. *Ranger* and a group of escort carriers provided the air cover for the all-American Western Task Force, which was ordered to secure Casablanca and the flanking Moroccan coast. *Ranger*'s air group comprised forty-four F4F-3 Wildcat fighters of VF-9 and VF-41, together with eighteen SBD dive-bombers of VS-41. In this view of some of VF-9s Wildcats, plane captains wait with their aircraft while the pilots receive a briefing before departing to patrol over the beach heads. Note the overlarge US ensign being flown at the masthead in the hope (mistaken) that Vichy French forces would not oppose an American landing. Also visible is the large CXAM radar antenna with the smaller YE homing beacon aerial above it.

Above: Douglas SBD Dauntless dive-bombers of VS-41 being positioned for a strike mission during Operation Torch. During 8 and 9 November, the SBDs were constantly employed in attacks on French destroyers and submarines that sortied against the US forces, and scored several hits. A particular problem was the partially complete Vichy battleship *Jean Bart*, which engaged the US ships at long range with the 15-in guns in her single operational turret. On the afternoon of 9 November, nine SBDs attacked the vessel, scoring two hits which caused the guns to cease firing. It is interesting to note that the SBD did not feature folding wings and consequently great care needed to be exercised when positioning the aircraft on a crowded flight deck.

Opposite above: A Grumman F4F-3 taking off from the USS *Ranger* during Operation Torch. Note the prominent yellow ring around the national markings, an identifying feature applied to all US aircraft employed in the operation. *Ranger*'s Wildcats saw a considerable amount of action, particularly on 8 November when eighteen Wildcats of VF-41 tangled with a mix of sixteen French Dewoitine D.520 and Curtiss 75A Hawks over Les Cazes airfield. This resulted in eight of the French aircraft being shot down for the loss of four Wildcats (including two brought down by ground fire). *Ranger*'s aircraft then destroyed another fourteen on the ground. Combined, these actions effectively ended French aerial opposition and the Wildcats subsequently concentrated on supporting ground troops and strafing any French ships attempting to attack the task force.

Opposite below: Accompanying *Ranger* as part of TF.34 were four Sangamon class escort carriers. Shown here is USS *Santee* (AVG-29) in the foreground with USS *Sangamon* (AVG-26) behind as they prepare to sail at the end of October 1942. *Santee*'s air group includes fourteen Wildcats (VGF-29) as well as 8 TBF Avengers and 9 SBD Dauntless (VGS-29) while *Sangamon* has a similar complement made up of VGF-26 and VGS-26. The 11,400-ton Sangamon class were converted from US Navy tankers during 1942 and they commissioned just in time to provide much-needed air support for Operation Torch. A third ship, USS *Suwannee* (AVG-27), was also part of TF.34 and carried a total of twenty-nine Wildcats as well as nine TBF Avengers. *NARA*

Above: The reason that *Suwannee* carried so many Wildcat fighters was that she embarked an additional squadron (VGF-28) from her sister ship USS *Chenango* (AVG-28). This was because *Chenango* was earmarked to act as a ferry carrier for the seventy-six Curtiss P-40 Warhawks of the USAAF 33rd Fighter Group, which are here shown tightly packed on the flight deck. In the background can be seen ships of Convoy UGF.1, which would carry US troops and their equipment to North Africa. *NARA*

Opposite above: With her flight deck covered with P-40s, the only way for the Air Force fighters to get airborne was by means of a catapult launch, as demonstrated here by the lead aircraft as others prepare to follow. The P-40s were lightly loaded as they only needed enough fuel to fly to the nearby airfield of Port Lyautey, which would be their base ashore. All the P-40s were successfully launched on 10 November and landed safely at the airfield. *Chenango* was then able to re-embark her Wildcats of VGF-28 from their temporary home aboard USS *Suwannee*.

Opposite below: After the conclusion of Operation Torch, *Ranger* returned to the US for a refit and then carried out two ferry trips bringing a total of 150 USAAF P-40 fighters to reinforce the 325th and 58th Fighter Groups in North Africa. Later she rejoined the British Home Fleet at Scapa Flow and on 4 October 1943, escorted by British units including the battleships HMS *Duke of York* and *Anson*, she arrived off the Norwegian coast and launched a series of strikes against German-controlled shipping at Bodø. At least five ships were sunk or damaged beyond repair. One of the main targets was the tanker *Schleswig*, visible under the nose of one of *Ranger's* SBDs flown by VB-4, as she was carrying oil fuel destined for the *Tirpitz* anchored further north at Alten Fjord, but although hit by at least one bomb, she was relatively undamaged. This was *Ranger's* last operational mission and for the rest of the war she was engaged on training and ferry duties. *NHIC*

Although no aircraft carriers were deployed in direct support of the D-Day landings at Normandy on 6 June 1944 (Operation Overlord), US cruisers and battleships provided fire support to the Allied troops as they went ashore. Normally, the ship's Curtiss SOC Seagull or Vought OS2U Kingfisher floatplanes would be used in the spotting role for naval gunfire but these were landed and stored ashore in preparation for D-Day. Instead the pilots were issued with British Supermarine Spitfires Mk.Vc to form VCS-7, which operated from airfields ashore. This had been found necessary following experience in Sicily and Italy, where the floatplanes had proved vulnerable to enemy fighters. US Navy mechanics here check over one of the Spitfires (still in British markings but carrying the D-Day stripes) between sorties.

Landings in the South of France (Operation Dragoon) began on 15 August 1944, but this time air support was provided by no fewer than seven escort carriers which between them carried over 200 fighters. Five of the carriers were British but two US carriers were also involved – USS *Kasaan Bay* (CVE-69) and USS *Tulagi* (CVE-72). This view taken from *Tulagi* shows the ships of Task Force 88.2 en route to the landings and in the background are three other carriers – USS *Kasaan Bay*, HMS *Hunter* and HMS *Stalker*. Aboard *Tulagi* can be seen some of the F6F Hellcats of VOF-1, and the unusual designation of this squadron relates to the fact that their primary task was observation duties for naval gunfire support. In practice, they became involved in reconnaissance missions and air strikes in support of ground troops, and in the course of these they shot down at least five enemy aircraft.

Above: Even before Pearl Harbor, the US Navy realised that many small aircraft carriers would be needed to supplement the larger fleet carriers, and in the spring of 1941, initiated the conversion of a standard diesel-powered C3 merchant vessel. The result was the USS *Long Island* (initially designated AVG-1), which had a short (360ft) flight deck and a single hanger aft. Commissioned June 1941, her significance was that she established the precedent of using merchant ship hulls to rapidly produce new carriers. Eventually, US shipyards delivered no fewer than 124 escort carriers, including thirty-eight for the Royal Navy. This aerial view shows *Long Island* as completed with a relatively short flight deck, which subsequently was lengthened by 60 feet over the bow. Interestingly, ranged on deck are two Brewster F3A-3 Buffalos of VS-201, one of the few Navy squadrons to fly this type from carriers.

Opposite above: The USS *Long Island* was the first of six similar vessels, of which four were handed over to the Royal Navy. They were followed by twenty-one Bogue class, of which eleven were transferred to the Royal Navy. The name ship, USS *Bogue* (CVE-9), was commissioned in September 1942 and immediately allocated to the first US Navy hunter killer group, which became operational in February 1943 – just in time to play an important role in the critical convoy battles of March and April 1943. During the rest of the war, *Bogue* and her associated escort groups were responsible for sinking thirteen U-boats. This view shows her at Bermuda in February 1945 with TBM Avengers of her air group on deck. *NHIC*

Opposite below: Following Operation Torch, most of the Sangamon class escort carriers involved were sent to the Pacific. However, the USS *Santee* (AVG-29/CVE-29) was retained, and after a short refit was deployed in the South Atlantic and later off the Bay of Biscay carrying out anti-submarine patrols. At that time (November 1943), her air group comprised eleven F4F-4 Wildcats of VF-29 and nineteen TBF-1C Avengers of VC-29. *Santee* was to have an eventful career. Moving to the Pacific in the spring of 1944, during the Battle of Leyte Gulf (October 1944) she was hit by a kamikaze and torpedoed by a Japanese submarine. Nevertheless, she was soon repaired and back in action.

By mid-1943, the US Navy had four hunter-killer groups in the Central and South Atlantic, each formed around an escort carrier. Apart from *Santee* and *Bogue*, there were also the carriers USS *Card* (CV-11) and USS *Core* (CV-13), and these quickly proved their worth. On 13 July 1943, a TBM Avenger of VC-13 from USS *Core* (shown here) attacked and damaged U-487, which was subsequently sunk by other aircraft. The next day, the same pilot (Lieutenant R.P. Williams USN) attacked U-527, although it was not sunk, but on 16 July he dropped four depth charges in a single pass over U-67, which sank immediately. In fact, in July 1943, US Navy ships and aircraft were involved in the destruction of no fewer than twenty-two U-boats. *NHIC*

The battle against the U-boats was also conducted by long-range shore-based maritime patrol aircraft. In mid-1943, responsibility for such operations passed from the USAAF to the US Navy and by the end of the year, aircraft of Fleet Air Wing (CFAW) Seven were based in Canada, Greenland, Iceland and the UK. These included Consolidated P4Y-1 Liberators, which had entered service in small numbers from August 1942 but were boosted in late 1943 by the transfer of USAAF B-24 Liberators. This is a PB4Y-1 flown by VB-103, which, in August 1943, was based at RAF St Eval, Cornwall, but later transferred to RAF Dunkeswell, Devon, where it remained until June 1945, and during that time was involved in the confirmed sinking of at least five U-boats.

Above: To cover the South Atlantic, VP-107 attached to CFAW-16 was equipped with PB4Ys and based at Natal in Northeast Brazil. On 5 November 1943, one of these aircraft surprised U-848 on the surface some 290 miles south-west of Ascension Island and launched an attack that damaged the U-boat so that it could not submerge. Two more squadron PB4Ys joined the fight and sank the submarine with two very accurate depth charge attacks. This dramatic view, taken from the tail turret of one of the aircraft that has just flown low over the U-boat during the course of the attacks, shows the German sailors vainly manning the twin 37mm and 20mm AA guns. U-848 was a Type IXD$_2$ U-boat on her first wartime patrol and all sixty-three of her crew were lost.

Opposite above: Supplementing the PB4Ys were numerous squadrons equipped with the twin-engined Lockheed PV-1 Ventura, a development of the Lockheed Hudson, which had been produced to meet an RAF specification and had entered service with Coastal Command in 1939. Some twenty Hudsons were diverted from British orders and served with US Navy squadron VP-82 from October 1941 as a stopgap until the much-improved PV-1 Ventura became available from December 1942. By September 1943, at least fifteen US Navy squadrons were equipped with the Ventura at bases along the US East Coast, in the Caribbean, and in Brazil, as well as one in North Africa.

Despite increasing use of land-based patrol bombers, the more traditional flying boats continued to make a major contribution to the war against the U-boats. Although the PBY Catalina was still widely used, by 1943 the majority of the flying boat squadrons operating over the Atlantic were equipped with the larger and more capable Martin PBM Mariner. The prototype XPBM-1 first flew in February 1939 and production PBM-1s entered service with VP-74 during 1941. An improved version was the PBM-3, which entered service in mid-1942 and could be identified by having fixed-wing floats (as opposed to retractable floats on the PBM-1). This is a PBM-3 of VP-211, which was formed in February 1943 but in the September was relocated to various bases in Brazil, where it remained almost until the end of the war. In this view, the iconic Sugar Loaf Mountain at Rio de Janeiro makes a prominent background feature.

As well as long-range patrol aircraft and flying boats, the Navy built up a significant force of inshore and coastal patrol squadrons, most of which were equipped with the single-engined Vought OS2U Kingfisher, which began to enter service in 1940. Initially allocated as observation floatplanes aboard the Pacific Fleet battleships, from late 1941 they began to equip East Coast Inshore Patrol squadrons, and by September 1943, there were no fewer than eighteen such squadrons deployed with the Atlantic Fleet. This is an OS2U-3 in 1941 era markings, one of 1,006 Kingfishers delivered up to 1942, while the Naval Aircraft Factory built another 300. Note the depth charges carried on the underwing racks.

Chapter 7

Hard Times

After the Midway and Coral Sea battles, the emphasis moved to the South Pacific, where in August 1942 it was observed that the Japanese were constructing an airfield on Guadalcanal, one of the most southerly of the Solomon Islands. This was part of a build-up aimed at the complete occupation of New Guinea and Port Moresby, and possibly onwards to Australia. Obviously this had to be prevented and, on 7 August, Operation Watchtower was launched, under which US Marines landed on Guadalcanal under cover of a naval task force which included the carriers *Enterprise*, *Saratoga* and *Wasp*. The stage was now set for some of the most intense fighting of the whole war and it was not until February 1943 that Guadalcanal was entirely in the hands of US forces.

While the fighting ashore ebbed and flowed, the US Navy's mission was to support the troops ashore and try to prevent Japanese reinforcements reaching the island. This was no easy task and resulted in no fewer than seven major naval engagements, including two carrier battles. Towards the end of August, a Japanese carrier task force approached the area with the objective of seeking out and destroying the US carriers. In the ensuing Battle of the Eastern Solomons on 24 August, the Japanese light carrier *Ryūjō* was sunk, but *Enterprise* was severely damaged and was under repair for two months.

While *Enterprise* was away, the *Saratoga* was also put out of action for three months after being torpedoed by a Japanese submarine on 31 August. Two weeks later, the USS *Wasp* was also torpedoed and quickly sank. *Saratoga*'s place was taken by the USS *Hornet* (CV-8), but with the loss of the *Wasp* she was the only US carrier available in the South Pacific for several weeks. In October 1942, the Japanese Fleet again mounted a major operation which was intended to capitalise on a successful advance by the Japanese Army on Guadalcanal. However, the Army advance stalled and the resulting delay just allowed time for the repaired *Enterprise* to join the US task force in time for the Battle of the Santa Cruz Islands. This was a hard-fought affair in which *Hornet* was sunk and *Enterprise* again damaged. In return, US aircraft sank the light carrier *Zuihō* and severely damaged the large carrier *Shōkaku*. Not immediately apparent to the US Navy was that in these carrier battles, and other actions, the Japanese had lost dozens of highly trained and experienced aircrew which they were never able to completely replace.

Although badly damaged at Santa Cruz, the *Enterprise* was patched up locally but remained as the only US carrier available in the area. *Saratoga* rejoined in late 1942 and in the New Year, the escort carriers USS *Suwannee* and USS *Chenango*, fresh from their involvement in Operation Torch, also arrived. For the rest of 1943 these carriers supported operations in New Guinea and advances through the Solomon Islands and New Britain. For a short period, the British carrier HMS *Victorious* replaced the *Enterprise*, which was withdrawn in May 1943 for a much-needed refit. Subsequently, as Japanese-held islands and their air bases were occupied by US troops, land-based air power was able to cover most of the amphibious operations, and events elsewhere meant that Japanese carriers were unlikely to intervene.

As far as the carrier war was concerned, the focus was now moving to the Central Pacific, where the US Pacific Fleet based at Pearl Harbor was steadily building its strength in preparation for a series of advances along the road to Japan. By mid-1943, the fleet was receiving the first of the new Essex class carriers as well as numbers of the Independence class light carriers. In addition, the fleet was receiving new aircraft that offered improved performance and greater offensive capability. The stage was being set for some of the most climactic battles of the war and ones that would ultimately lead to the defeat of Japan.

Opposite below: Air support for Operation Watchtower, which commenced on 7 August 1942, was provided by Task Force 61, which was organised into three groups, each comprising a carrier with an escort of two cruisers and several destroyers. Group 2, centred on the USS *Enterprise* (CV-6), also included the new battleship USS *North Carolina* (BB-55). In this image taken on 24 July during rehearsals for the landings, LCP(L) landing craft carrying elements 1st US Marine Corps Division manoeuvre prior to commencing an assault. In the foreground are aircraft of VB-6, one of two SBD Dauntless-equipped squadrons aboard the *Enterprise* (the other was VS-5). Also on board at the time were F4F Wildcats of VF-6 and TBF Avengers of VT-3.

Only a month after Pearl Harbor, the carrier USS *Saratoga* (CV-3) had been torpedoed by a Japanese submarine on 11 January 1942 and consequently had not been available when the Coral Sea and Midway battles had been fought. However, in July 1942 she moved to the South West Pacific area and combined with the carriers *Enterprise* and *Wasp* to form TF.61. While undergoing a substantial refit following the torpedo damage, her original main armament of deck-mounted 8-in guns was replaced by a much more useful battery of eight 5-in/38 cal dual-purpose guns in four twin mountings. In addition, the light AA armament was increased, new radars fitted and the hull modified with anti-torpedo bulges. Some of these changes can be seen in this view of the ship as she headed south to her new assignment and first taste of action.

For Operation Watchtower, *Saratoga*'s Air Group 3 comprised VF-5 with thirty-four F4F Wildcats, VB-3 and VS-3 with a total of thirty-four SBD Dauntless, and VT-8 with fifteen of the new TBF Avengers for a total of eighty-three aircraft. In this view, one of the TBFs that has just landed is passing the huge funnel on which are now stowed several large life rafts. On the morning of 7 August, Air Group 3 mounted strikes against Japanese targets on Guadalcanal, and in the afternoon, VF-5 waded into a formation of eleven Aichi 99 (Val) dive-bombers and claimed ten of them as shot down. Over the two days of fighting, *Saratoga* recorded 354 take-offs but lost seven F4Fs and one SBD (although only five were due to enemy action), against which a total of twelve enemy aircraft were claimed. *NHIC*

The airfield on Guadalcanal, which had triggered Operation Watchtower, became the main objective of the invasion force and was captured on the first day. However, it was not available for use until 12 August, and even then was under regular attack by Japanese ground, air and naval forces for several weeks afterwards. Despite that, Wildcats and Dauntless dive-bombers operated by US Marine squadrons were flown in from the escort carrier USS *Long Island* on 20 August, and the airfield was regularly used as a staging and refuelling point by various carrier-based units. It was named Henderson Field, in memory of Major Lofton Henderson USMC, who was killed in action in the Battle of Midway. This view shows the airfield towards the end of August, shortly after becoming operational.

The scene aboard USS *Wasp* (CV-7) during the morning of 7 August, when the ship was supporting the Guadalcanal landings. Facing the camera (wearing binoculars) is Rear Admiral Leigh Noyes (commanding TG.61.1) and to his left, wearing a helmet, is Captain Forrest P. Sherman, the ship's commanding officer. Over the two days of the operation, *Wasp* launched 312 sorties and only four aircraft were lost, of which two were due to enemy action. In strikes against Japanese forces her aircraft dropped sixty-seven 1,000lb bombs, fifty 500lb bombs and sixteen 325lb depth charges. The latter were actually used as conventional bombs as an SBD could carry three at a time instead of a single 1,000lb or 500lb bomb. On deck, several SBDs are here being prepared for another strike.

Apart from their success in the Battle of Savo Island and the landing of a small force of troops (which were almost immediately wiped out by the US Marines), the Japanese high command was slow to respond to the US invasion of Guadalcanal. It was not until 23 August that a major naval task force, including the carriers *Shōkaku*, *Zuikaku* and *Ryūjō*, was approaching the area under the overall command of Admiral Nagumo. Unfortunately, incorrect intelligence misled Admiral Fletcher as to the position of the Japanese carriers and he judged it safe to detach *Wasp* for refuelling. Thus, on the morning of 24 August, when the Japanese force was spotted approaching from the north and the Battle of the Eastern Solomons opened, he only had *Enterprise* and *Saratoga* (here with *Enterprise* in the background) on hand.

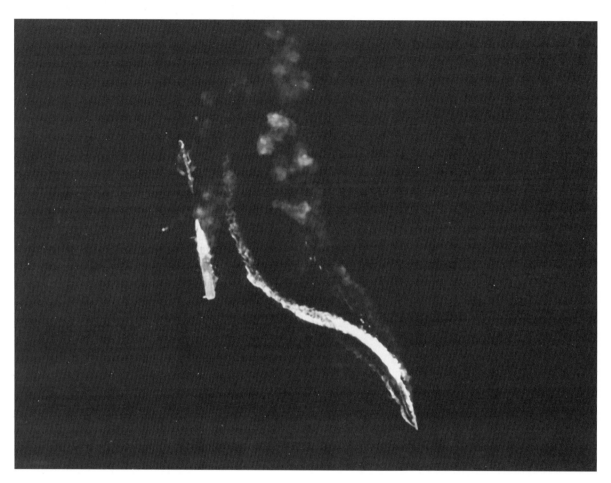

The first Japanese force to be spotted was the *Ryūjō* group, which was subsequently attacked by the Dauntless of VS-3 and VB-3, as well as Avengers of VT-8, from *Saratoga*. The Japanese carrier was hit by at least four bombs and a torpedo, and was left in a sinking condition, although she stayed afloat for another six hours before finally going down. This gave time for the destroyers *Amatsukaze* and *Tokitsukaze* to close and take off survivors, and they can be seen moving away from the crippled carrier in this photo taken from a USAAF B-17 Fortress, which was part of a subsequent, but unsuccessful, high-level attack (note the pattern of bomb bursts on the right).

While the *Ryūjō* was under attack, Nagumo had already located the US carriers and had launched a strike in two waves. These fought their way through a CAP of around fifty Wildcats and succeeded in hitting *Enterprise* with three bombs, as well as several damaging near misses. This dramatic image captures the moment when a Val dive-bomber burst into flames as it was hit by AA fire while attempting to dive onto the *Enterprise*. The carrier itself, although unable to operate aircraft, was saved by the Herculean damage-control efforts of her crew but was forced to withdraw, eventually to Pearl Harbor, for repairs. Strikes launched earlier from *Enterprise* failed to find the Japanese carriers and in due course recovered to *Saratoga* or ashore to Henderson Field. Faced with the prospect of renewed attacks by Japanese carrier and land-based aircraft, Fletcher wisely withdrew to the south having at least thwarted the superior Japanese in its objectives.

Following the Eastern Solomons, Fletcher still had the carriers *Saratoga* and *Wasp* available to provide support for the Marines ashore on Guadalcanal. However, on 31 August, the USS *Saratoga* was hit by a torpedo fired by the Japanese submarine I-26 when some 260 miles south-east of Guadalcanal. Initially brought to a standstill, she eventually got underway but later returned to Pearl Harbor for repairs and did not come back to the South Pacific area until the end of November. Another tragedy occurred on 15 September, when the USS *Wasp* was torpedoed and sunk by the Japanese submarine I-19 while escorting a convoy of troop reinforcements to Guadalcanal. Hit by three torpedoes, the carrier was quickly engulfed in flames and secondary explosions, as seen here from an accompanying destroyer, and the order to abandon ship was given only thirty-five minutes after the attack, in which 193 men were killed but 1,946 were saved (including over 300 wounded).

With *Saratoga* out of action, and *Wasp* sunk, the newly arrived USS *Hornet* (CV-8) was the only carrier available in the South West Pacific area. In October 1942, the Japanese began a major offensive on Guadalcanal, planning to capture Henderson Field on Y-Day, 22 October. Anticipating this, Yamamoto ordered virtually the entire Combined Fleet, including five carriers, to sea and to be ready to move in once the threat of air attack from the airfield was eliminated. However, the US Marines were not party to this plan and stubbornly held out, allowing time for the recently repaired USS *Enterprise* to join up with *Hornet*. By dawn on the 26th, Admiral Kinkaid, who was in overall command of the American carriers, was aware of the presence of the Japanese carriers some 200 miles north-west. That morning, both sides launched large-scale strikes against the opposing carrier groups and the first Japanese wave concentrated on the *Hornet*, which was hit by four bombs and two torpedoes despite heavy AA fire and the efforts of the fighters overhead. This image is one of the most dramatic of the battle, showing the *Hornet* manoeuvring frantically as a Val dive-bomber plunges towards the ship.

Above: A second wave of Japanese aircraft selected the USS *Enterprise* as their target. Dodging torpedoes, she was hit by two bombs, but these did not materially affect her operational capacity and she continued in action. Instrumental in fighting off many of the attackers was the new battleship *South Dakota*, whose intense and accurate AA fire accounted for several enemy aircraft, and others were deflected from hitting the carrier. Here, *Enterprise* defends herself with heavy AA fire and *South Dakota* can be seen in the background. Later that morning, a second attack developed but *Enterprise* received no further damage, although one bomb hit the *South Dakota*'s forward 16-in gun turret.

Opposite above: Early on the morning of 26 October, *Enterprise* had launched sixteen SBDs of VS-10, which spread out searching for the Japanese forces. Two of these came across the small 11,250-ton carrier *Zuihō*. Without hesitation they piled in for the attack, achieved complete surprise, and placed two 500lb bombs squarely on the after flight deck, which put the carrier out of action for the rest of the battle (although she was subsequently repaired). Other VS-10 aircraft spotted the Admiral Nagumo's main force, which included the large 25,700-ton carriers *Shōkaku* and *Zuikaku*, and based on the sighting reports, Admiral Kinkaid immediately ordered his two carriers to launch strikes. *Hornet* launched two waves, which included twenty-four SBDs and fifteen TBFs escorted by fifteen F4F Wildcats. *Enterprise*'s effort was smaller due to the absence of the SBDs on the earlier scouting mission but still sent three SBDs and eight TBF Avengers. One of these is shown here about to take off while to one side, sailors are holding up hastily scrawled briefing boards, one of which gives updated information concerning the Japanese carriers and the other states 'Proceed without *Hornet*'.

Opposite below: In the late morning, *Enterprise* was attacked by a wave of dive-bombers followed by over a dozen B5N torpedo bombers. She was hit by three bombs, one of which put the forward lift out of action, but by skilful manoeuvring avoided all the torpedoes. In this view the flight deck crew are attempting to reposition Wildcats and Dauntless of CVG-10 while the ship heels violently to port as she turns away from the torpedo tracks. Note the two balls on the signal hoist indicating that the ship is 'Not Under Control'. *NARA*

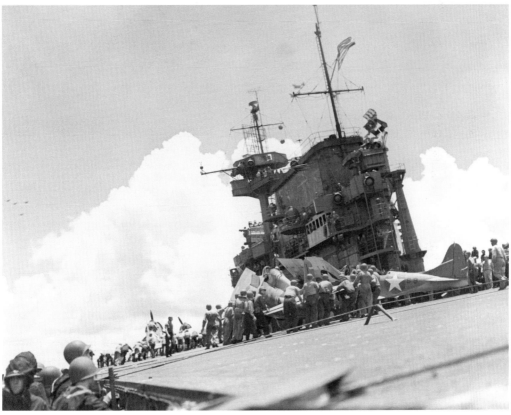

The SDBs of *Hornet*'s VS-8 managed to hit the *Shōkaku* with six bombs, causing a tremendous amount of damage and putting her out of action. Eventually, she made her way back to Japan but was under repair for nine months. With their own carrier out of action the surviving *Hornet* aircraft were recovered by the *Enterprise*. In the meantime, the fires aboard *Hornet* had been mostly extinguished and preparations were made for the cruiser *Northampton* to take her in tow while destroyers closed to take off some of the crew, as shown here. However, later that afternoon, further attacks resulted in another torpedo hit and damage from near miss bombs. Any hope of saving the ship was now gone and in the face of the approaching powerful Japanese surface fleet, the carrier was abandoned. Attempts by US destroyers to sink her by gunfire and torpedoes failed and the coup de grace was delivered by Japanese destroyers during the night.

With the loss of *Hornet*, the USS *Enterprise* remained as the only available US carrier in the South West Pacific. She retired briefly to Nouméa, New Caledonia, for repairs but put to sea again before these were completed in order to meet a strong Japanese force approaching Guadalcanal. This resulted in a series of engagements known as the Naval Battle of Guadalcanal, over several days (11–15 November 1942). Although two Japanese carriers were in the area, there was no direct action between the opposing carriers, but *Enterprise*'s VT-10, detached to Henderson Field, participated in the sinking of the Japanese battleship *Hiei* on 13 November and on the 14th attacked and damaged several Japanese heavy cruisers. In May 1943, she finally made her way back to Pearl Harbor for a much needed refit. Here, the aircraft of CVG-10 prepare to fly off as the ship approaches Hawaii accompanied by the battleship USS *Washington*. NHIC

Fortunately, *Enterprise*'s position as the only available carrier was short-lived as the USS *Saratoga*, her torpedo damage repaired, returned to the South Pacific towards the end of November. In January 1943, further reinforcements arrived in the form of the escort carriers USS *Suwannee* and USS *Chenango*, which had been transferred to the Pacific theatre following their involvement in Operation Torch (November 1942). Their main role was to provide air cover for the numerous convoys bringing fresh troops and supplies to Guadalcanal but they were not suitable for fleet operations due to their slow speed (18 knots) and limited facilities. However, they each carried an air group of around thirty aircraft made up of F4F Wildcats, SBD Dauntless (*Chenango* only) and TBF Avengers. Some of the latter are here, making a low pass over one of the escorts, with the two carriers visible astern. *NHIC*

In 1943, while the battle-tried *Enterprise* and *Saratoga* were holding the ring against Japanese advances in the South Pacific, the Pacific Fleet at Pearl Harbor was starting to receive new generations of carriers, which would eventually spearhead an advance across the Pacific to Japan itself. The first Essex class carriers had been ordered as early as September 1940 and the lead ship (USS *Essex*, CV-9) commissioned on 31 December 1942. After trials and operational training she joined the Pacific Fleet in May 1943 and is shown here at that time alongside at Pearl Harbor. At 27,000 tons, these ships were larger than the Yorktown class (20,000 tons) and were capable of operating up to 100 aircraft. By the end of 1943, no fewer than five Essex class were available for operations.

Opposite above: It wasn't just new ships that were joining the fleet. Until mid-1943, the sole US Navy fighter in action was the Grumman F4F Wildcat. While it was a tough and reliable aircraft, it lacked the speed and manoeuvrability of the Japanese A6M Zero. Despite this, US Navy pilots put up some very creditable performances in combat once they had evolved suitable tactics to overcome the differences. However, the fighter squadrons aboard the Essex class carriers introduced the new F6F Hellcat, which was to become the standard US Navy fighter for the rest of the war. Compared to the Wildcat, the new fighter was some 60mph faster and had a much improved rate of climb. Later versions also proved capable of carrying two 1,000lb bombs and so could be used as powerful fighter bombers. The first squadron to receive the new fighters was VF-9 aboard the USS *Essex*, where they are shown in May 1943 preparing for take-off.

Opposite below: In July 1943, a second Essex class carrier joined the Pacific Fleet at Pearl Harbor. This was the USS *Yorktown* (CV-10), one of several new carriers that commemorated the names of ships lost earlier in the war. Her air group (CVG-5) comprised no fewer than ninety-three aircraft made up of VF-6 with thirty-six of the new F6F Hellcats, VB-6 with thirty-six SBD Dauntless dive-bombers, and VT-6 with eighteen TBF Avengers. An additional F6F was allocated to the air group commander (CAG). By this stage of the war the Grumman TBF Avenger (alternatively designated as the TBM when produced under subcontract by the Eastern Aircraft division of General Motors) was widely deployed with the fleet, having supplanted the TBD Devastator, which was withdrawn from front-line use in the immediate aftermath of the Battle of Midway. Here, TBFs are in the process of being ranged aft on *Yorktown*'s flight deck in October 1943.

After Pearl Harbor, the previously discarded idea of converting cruiser hulls to aircraft carriers was revisited and subsequently, nine Cleveland class cruisers then under construction were earmarked for conversion while still on the slipway. The result was the nine light fleet carriers of the Independence class, all of which entered service during 1943. The first two, USS *Independence* (CVL-22) and USS *Princeton* (CVL-23), joined the Pacific Fleet at Pearl Harbor in July and August respectively, and this view shows the latter at that time with her air group of nine SBDs (VC-23) and twelve F6F Hellcats (VF-23) ranged aft. Although something of a compromise, the benefit of these light carriers was that they were quickly available and their cruiser machinery gave them a speed of over 31 knots, enabling them to operate as part of the new fast carrier task forces.

Above: As well as the ships that were lost in the fierce carrier battles of the first twelve months of the Pacific war, both sides lost many aircrew, including some of the most experienced, and how replacements were recruited and trained was to have a major effect on the conduct of future operations. On the US side, a major expansion of the training organisation had already begun. In 1940, only 708 new pilots had been trained but by 1942 this had risen to 10,869, and over 20,000 were trained in each of the following two years, numbers that the Japanese couldn't even approach due to lack of instructors, facilities and fuel. And it wasn't just numbers that counted. Each new US Navy pilot probably had at least 300 hours flight time when he reached his first squadron while their Japanese equivalents were lucky to have half that figure, and even less in the later stages of the war. This scene of activity at a Miami training airfield in 1942 gives some indication of the scale of the US effort. Apart from North American SNJ trainers, various fighters only recently withdrawn from front-line use such as the Grumman F3F and Brewster F2A Buffalo are being used for advanced training.

Opposite above: With Guadalcanal secured in the first week of February 1943, US forces began to take the offensive. Carrier support comprised the *Saratoga* and *Enterprise*, although the escort carriers *Chenango*, *Suwannee* and *Sangamon* were also available, but to provide cover for landings on New Georgia, *Saratoga* was joined by the Royal Navy carrier HMS *Victorious* at the end of May, the two ships forming the core of Task Group TG.36.3. *Victorious* is shown here after her arrival in Nouméa with Wildcats and Avengers ranged on deck. For the actual operations in June and July, the Avengers were transferred to *Saratoga* while most of the latter's Wildcats were transferred to the British carrier, which had better fighter control capabilities. The arrival of *Victorious* released the USS *Enterprise*, which had departed for a much overdue refit.

The Pacific fleet was boosted in September 1943 by the addition of another Essex class carrier, USS *Bunker Hill* (CV-17). Almost immediately, she joined with *Essex* (CV-9) and *Independence* (CVL-22) to form Task Group TG.50.3, which made a series of highly successful strikes against the Japanese base at Rabaul. When *Bunker Hill* was commissioned in April 1943, her air group included VF-17 equipped with the new Vought F4U Corsair but by the time the ship reached Pearl Harbor, the US Navy had decided that this aircraft was not suitable for carrier operations and the squadron was diverted to the Solomon Islands, where they flew from shore-based airfields. The photo shows one of the squadron's Corsairs displaying an impressive set of 'kill' symbols while based at Majuro in January 1944.

Bunker Hill (CV-17) was also the first carrier to operate the new Curtiss SB2C-1 Helldiver, which eventually would replace the long-serving SBD Dauntless in the course of the next eighteen months. Their first operational use was in the Rabaul raids on 2 November 1943, when they shared in the sinking of a Japanese destroyer and scored hits on three other destroyers and two cruisers. This view shows a pair of Helldivers of VB-17 joining the carrier's landing pattern, with two more ahead of them, one over the round-down and the next on base leg to follow. *NHIC*

In the Pacific, as in the Atlantic, the US Navy made extensive use of flying boats and these were almost exclusively Consolidated PBY Catalinas, which equipped at least eight Air Wings (CFAW). In September 1943, for example, FAW 1 covering the South Pacific area included four Catalina squadrons, each with around fifteen aircraft. Whereas in the Atlantic the flying boats were almost entirely employed on anti-submarine patrols, in the Pacific they carried out long-ranging scouting flights and, armed with bombs and torpedoes, attacked enemy surface vessels. Several Catalina squadrons employed on night attacks against Japanese shipping were painted black and acquired the nickname 'Black Cats'. These included VP-52 based at Port Moresby (New Guinea), and three of its radar-equipped PBY-5As are shown here in December 1943. *NHIC*

Chapter 8

Destination Japan

The advance across the Pacific began at the end of August 1943 with the occupation of the Ellice Islands to provide a base for US aircraft to support the next assaults against the Gilbert Islands (Operation Galvanic). Commencing on 20 November 1943, the main objectives were the islands of Makin and Tarawa; the latter in particular was a bloody affair. The impressive carrier task forces assembled to support these landings was in stark contrast to the critical situation at the end of 1942.

Once secured, the Gilbert Islands provided a stepping stone for Operation Flintlock, the occupation of the Marshall Islands in January and February 1944. Heeding the lessons of Tarawa, US casualties were much lighter, but again the Japanese garrisons fought almost literally to the last man. Subsequently, US forces moved on and occupied Kwajalein and Eniwetok, the former being an atoll enclosing one of the world's largest natural harbours, which became a forward base for further advances across the Pacific.

The next objectives were the Marianas, which included the large islands of Saipan, Tinian and Guam. Over 1,000 miles closer to Japan, the establishment of air bases on these would bring that country within range of USAAF strategic bombers. Operation Forager was launched on 17 June 1944 and the reaction of the Japanese Combined Fleet resulted in what was the most decisive carrier engagement of the war, the Battle of the Philippine Sea. The Japanese carrier fleet had been regenerated to some extent and could field nine carriers with 473 aircraft embarked, with additional support available from aircraft based on Guam. However, the US Task Force 58 could field almost twice as many carriers, with 956 aircraft embarked. The outcome was an outright victory for the US fliers, who claimed 346 Japanese aircraft destroyed, and at the end of the day there were only thirty-five aircraft left aboard surviving Japanese carriers (three were sunk). This dramatic outcome was down to two main factors. The first was the radar-directed fighter control system then established within the US task force, which enabled incoming enemy formations to be intercepted long before reaching their targets. The other was the poor standard of the Japanese aircrew who had replaced earlier losses and lacked both training and experience.

The invasion of the Philippines in October 1944 precipitated the Battle of Leyte Gulf. By that time the remaining Japanese carriers lacked both aircraft and pilots and were reduced to acting as a decoy force, a role it performed successfully although in the process losing four carriers to overwhelming US air attacks. However, this sacrifice allowed a strong Japanese force, including the mighty battleship *Yamato*, to debauch unchallenged through the San Bernardino Strait and fall upon the escort carriers of TF.77.4.3 (Taffy 3). One of these was sunk (USS *Gambier Bay* (CVE-73)), as well as three destroyers, before the Japanese force retired under constant air attack from aircraft flown from the other escort carriers, including those of Taffy 2. US ships now came under an entirely new form of attack and the escort carrier *St. Lo* (CVE-63) gained the dubious distinction of being the first ship to be sunk by kamikaze attack.

By January 1945, the fast carriers of Task Force 58 demonstrated their ability to roam at will in wide-ranging sorties in the South China Sea in which its aircraft attacked targets in Indochina (now Vietnam), Formosa (Taiwan) and Honshu (one of the Japanese homeland Islands). This was a preliminary to Operation Detachment, the invasion of Iwo Jima in February 1945, followed by Operation Iceberg, when US forces landed on Okinawa. Japanese forces reacted strongly to these events and the US fleet was subjected to an intense series of kamikaze and conventional attacks in which the carriers of TF.58 were the principal targets.

Following the Leyte Gulf battle, the Japanese Combined Fleet had ceased to exist as a credible fighting force, although on 6 April 1945, the battleship *Yamato*, accompanied by a light cruiser and several destroyers, sortied from the Inland Sea on a one-way mission to attack the US amphibious force gathered off Okinawa. The following day she was caught by 380 aircraft from the carriers of TG.58.1 and TG.58.3, which attacked in two waves. The result was a foregone conclusion and the *Yamato* went down in a hail of bombs and torpedoes, taking her crew of almost 3,000 men with her.

In the closing stages of the war the carriers of Task Force 38 (now under Admiral Halsey) ranged off the coast of Japan in preparation for Operation Olympic, which would have been the final assault on Japan itself, planned for November 1945. For this the US Navy would have been able to deploy five carrier task groups, including no fewer than fourteen Essex class carriers as well as the veteran USS *Enterprise* – a staggering comparison with the state of affairs in the immediate aftermath of Pearl Harbor in 1941. Of course, the dropping of the atomic bombs brought the war to a sudden and unexpected end and the final demonstration of US naval air power was a peaceful massed formation flypast over Tokyo Bay on 2 September 1945, when the formal surrender documents were signed aboard the USS *Missouri*.

Above: The eventual ability of the Fast Carrier Task Force to roam almost at will across the Pacific relied heavily on an extensive and well-organised fleet train. Here, the Independence class light fleet carrier USS *Cowpens* (CVL-25) is taking on fuel from the fleet oiler USS *Platte* (AO-24) in November 1943. At that time, US forces were mounting the first major offensive action in the Central Pacific, the objectives being Tarawa and Makin in the Gilbert Islands. *Cowpens* (affectionately known to her crew as the *'Mighty Moo'*) was part of TG.50.1, which was stationed north of Makin Island to protect the invasion forces against enemy air and surface incursions from the Marshall Islands and the Truk naval base.

Opposite above: At the end of 1943, the Fast Carrier Force was reorganised as Task Force 58 under the command of Rear Admiral (later Vice-Admiral) Marc Mitscher and its first action was Operation Flintlock in January 1944. The objectives were the strategically important Marshall Islands, which included the massive natural harbour at Kwajalein Atoll. The carriers available to TF.58 were organised into four groups and included four Essex class, *Saratoga* and *Enterprise*, and six Independence class. TG.58.3 comprised the USS *Bunker Hill* (CV-17) and light fleet carriers *Monterey* (CVL-26) and *Cowpens* (CVL-25). Here, the latter's Hellcats of VF-25 prepare to take off for strikes against Kwajalein. Ranged aft are TBF Avengers of VT-25.

Opposite below: The USS *Enterprise* (CV-6) was one of the stalwarts of the Pacific War, participating in almost all the major actions, and was under repair following a kamikaze attack when the war ended. In January 1944, she was attached to TF.58.1 covering the occupation of the Marshall Islands, when this TBF Avenger belonging to VT-10 is shown about to land aboard. The aircraft is finished in the then standard blue/grey/white colour scheme introduced in 1943, but at this time has no distinguishing air group markings on the tail. At left, the LDO (Landing Deck Officer) watches after having successfully guided the pilot to the point of touchdown.

By midsummer 1944, Task Force 58 included no fewer than six Essex class carriers, as well as the veteran USS *Enterprise* (CV-6) and eight Independence class. These would be supplemented in the forthcoming operations to occupy the Marianas by numerous escort carriers, which provided anti-submarine escort, close support for troops ashore and acted as aircraft ferries. This view looking aft from the USS *Essex* shows the light fleet carrier USS *San Jacinto* (CVL-30) and USS *Wasp* (CV-18) as ships of TF.58 carry out training exercises in May 1944. Aircraft on deck are the SB2C Helldivers of VB-15 and TBF/TBM Avengers of VT-15. Just visible on the tail fin of the Helldivers is the single horizontal white stripe that was the distinguishing mark of the carrier's Air Group 15.

Operation Forager precipitated the greatest naval air battle of the Pacific War. On 19 June 1944, the Japanese Mobile Fleet commanded by Admiral Ozawa launched 358 aircraft in four waves for a series of strikes against the ships of the US Task Force 58. Radar warnings enabled squadrons of Hellcats to intercept them so that very few got through to attempt attacks on individual ships and very little damage was done. During the course of the day, US fighters or AA fire accounted for no fewer than 346 Japanese aircraft (including some operating from airfields ashore) for the loss of only thirty US aircraft. Picking up on a phrase used by one of the fighter pilots describing the action, it became known as the 'Great Marianas Turkey Shoot'. Here, an F6F-3 Hellcat of VF-1 (Top Hatters) prepares to take off from USS *Yorktown* to intercept an incoming raid, information for which is displayed on a board held up by one of the crew.

Opposite: Following the decisive defeat of the Japanese strikes against TF.58 on 19 June 1944, the next day, US scout planes located the Japanese Mobile Fleet some 300 miles to the west. Late in the afternoon the US carriers launched a strike made up of 131 Avengers, Dauntless and Helldivers escorted by eighty-five Hellcat fighters. This included these SB2C Helldivers of VB-1 from the USS *Yorktown* (CV-10), some of which attacked and seriously damaged the Japanese carrier *Zuikaku*. By the time the strike force had completed the 600-mile round trip they were running low on fuel and it was dark. Admiral Mitscher ordered all ships to display their lights to assist the fliers as they approached their carriers. Even so, of the fifty-one Helldivers that took part in the mission, no fewer than thirty-six were forced to ditch or were lost in deck landing accidents, although many of the ditched aircrew were subsequently picked up.

In major operations such as the invasion of Saipan in the Marianas, escort carriers played a number of essential supporting roles, one of which was to ferry USAAF aircraft which could subsequently be flown ashore to newly captured or constructed airfields. In this case, the USS *Manila Bay* (CVE-61) has carried the Republic P-47 Thunderbolts of the 73rd Fighter Squadron (318th FG), which are now preparing to fly off to Saipan on 24 June, only a few days after the initial landings. Once ashore these and other units would take over responsibility for the air defence of the islands, thus releasing the carriers of TF.58 for other operations.

Although by 1944 the Grumman F4F Wildcat had been replaced by the more capable F6F Hellcat aboard the fleet carriers, it still equipped units allocated to many escort carriers and continued to do so until the end of the war. However, Wildcat production was transferred to the Eastern Aircraft Division of General Motors and aircraft from this source were designated FM-1. From September 1943, it was succeeded by the FM-2, in which the original 1,200hp Pratt & Whitney Twin Wasp engine was replaced by a 1,350hp Wright Cyclone. The two examples shown here were operating from the USS *White Plains* (CVE-66), which formed part of TG.52.14.1 supporting the landings on Saipan and Tinian in June and July 1944.

After Operation Forager, command of the US 5th Fleet, including Task Force 58, passed from Admiral Raymond Spruance to Admiral 'Bull' Halsey and became the 3rd Fleet, while the Fast Carrier Task Force was redesignated TF.38. This arrangement allowed Spruance and his staff to plan for operations against Iwo Jima and Okinawa while Halsey could plan and execute the assault on the Philippines, and later also conducted the final operations against the Japanese homeland islands. However, throughout these changes, command and tactical direction of the fast carriers as either TF.38 or TF.58 remained with Vice-Admiral Marc Mitscher, who established a reputation as the supreme exponent of carrier airpower, remaining in post until the end of the war. This portrait shows him on the flag bridge of USS *Randolph* (CV-15) together with his chief of staff, Commodore Arleigh Burke, during operations off Okinawa in June 1945. *NHIC*

As a preliminary to the invasion of the Philippines, in October 1944 a series of raids against Formosa and the Ryukyu Islands were carried out by Task Force 38 with the objective of destroying Japanese aircraft that might otherwise oppose the Leyte landings. This SB2C Helldiver of VB-7 is joining the landing circuit of its carrier, USS *Hancock* (CV-19) after returning from a successful strike against a Formosan airfield. Note the inverted horseshoe symbol carried by aircraft of the ship's air group, CVG-7. By this period of the war, the Helldiver, with its heavy bomb load, was an increasingly important element of the US Navy's air power as the emphasis shifted to attacking land targets in support of ground operations. On the other hand, especially after Leyte Gulf, the need for a specialised anti-ship torpedo bomber virtually disappeared. Consequently, by August 1945, the TBM Avenger was being gradually withdrawn and it was planned that carrier air groups would consist only of fighters and Helldivers as, for example, was then the case aboard the USS *Lexington* (CV-16).

Landings on Leyte Gulf in the Philippines began on 20 October 1944 and produced a predictably strong response from Japanese aircraft based on Luzon. On 24 October, over eighty attacked the USS *Princeton* (CVL-23), part of TG.38.3 covering the landings, and although her Hellcats claimed at least twenty-eight shot down, a single D4Y Judy succeeded in hitting the ship with two 500lb bombs. These started major fires, which raged out of control. The cruiser USS *Birmingham* (CL-62) is shown coming alongside to evacuate some of the crew but subsequently, a huge explosion aboard the *Princeton* caused major damage to the cruiser, killing 233 of her crew – more than were eventually lost aboard the carrier. *Princeton* herself was eventually abandoned and sank after yet another large explosion.

Flagship of TG.38.3 was the USS *Essex*, which also came under attack at the same time as *Princeton* but managed to avoid any damage. Although the attacking force of around sixty Japanese aircraft was intercepted by only seven of the ship's Hellcats, they broke up the formation and shot down over two dozen. Indeed, one pilot, Commander David McCampbell, claimed nine 'kills' and his wingman, Lieutenant Roy Rushing, another six. Without taking away any credit from the American pilots, this outcome demonstrated the inexperience and lack of training of this generation of new Japanese pilots. In this scene, deck crew aboard the Essex rush to refuel and re-arm their Hellcats while the ship heels over as it manoeuvres to avoid attacks. In the background, an enemy aircraft burns, and in the distance is another carrier, probably USS *Lexington*.

Another carrier lost during the Leyte operations was the escort carrier USS *St. Lo* (CVE-63). She had initially commissioned in October 1943 as the USS *Midway* but a year later her name was changed to *St. Lo* to free up her original name for the first of a new class of large carriers then under construction. On 25 October 1944, the ship was part of TG.77.4.3 providing support for the troops ashore when she was hit by a kamikaze aircraft which penetrated the flight deck and detonated in the hanger, where ready use bombs and torpedoes were stored. The resultant explosion was enough to mortally damage the ship, which later sank, gaining the dubious distinction of being the first of many ships to be sunk by kamikaze attack.

In the immediate aftermath of the Leyte battles, Task Force 38 remained on station to support operations ashore in the Philippines. On 30 October 1944, TG.38.4, consisting of the carriers *Enterprise* (CV-6), *Franklin* (CV-13), *Belleau Wood* (CVL-24), and *San Jacinto* (CVL-30), mounted strikes against Japanese-held airfields around Manila. In response it suffered attacks by numerous kamikazes, which hit *Franklin* and *Belleau Wood*, both of which had to be withdrawn to Ulithi for repairs. Here, fire-fighting teams aboard *Belleau Wood* attempt to prevent fires engulfing the Avengers and Hellcats of CVLG-21 ranged on deck. In the background the USS *Franklin* is also on fire, although on this occasion the damage was eventually repaired and the ship was back in action. Unfortunately, in March 1945, off Okinawa, she was hit again and almost sunk, while 724 of her crew were killed and another 265 wounded.

Despite the defeat of the Imperial Japanese Navy at Leyte Gulf, the occupation of Luzon and the rest of the Philippines entailed months of heavy fighting ashore. Until USAAF squadrons were established ashore, air support remained the task of the TF.58 carriers. Here, Hellcats of VF-80 prepare to take off from the USS *Ticonderoga* (CV-14) to attack targets in Manila Bay on 5 November 1944. Of interest are the two leading Hellcats, which are radar-equipped F6F-5Ns, specialist night fighters that were playing an increasingly important role in the defence of the fleet. Subsequently, most fighter squadrons included a few examples in their overall strength.

Opposite above: In November 1944, the USS *Intrepid* (CV-11) was attached to TG.38.2.1, part of the force supporting operations in the Philippines. She also came under kamikaze attack at the end of October and ten of her crew were killed, although the ship remained on station. This photo was taken during the following November and shows aircraft of CVG-18 ranged aft. These include the then usual mix of Hellcats, Avengers and Helldivers, and of particular interest is that one of the Hellcats in front of the island superstructure is parked over the edge of the flight deck, with its tail supported by an outrigger strut. On 25 November, the ship was again attacked and hit by two kamikazes, starting fires and killing sixty-six men. Although the fires were quickly extinguished, *Intrepid* was withdrawn the next day and proceeded to San Francisco for repairs, which lasted until February 1945. *NHIC*

Opposite below: On 17 December 1944, Halsey's Task Force 38 was operating some 300 miles east of Luzon when it encountered Typhoon Cobra. Over the next two days, the ships experienced heavy seas and winds of up to 140mph. Three destroyers were lost and several of the carriers were damaged, some requiring major repairs. Some idea of the severity of the conditions can be gained from this photo taken aboard the USS *Anzio* (CVE-57), which at the time was part of an anti-submarine escort group. Lashed securely on deck is a TMB Avenger of VC-60 and the group of sailors on deck appear unperturbed by the ship's excessive angle of heel.

Landings on Iwo Jima (Operation Detachment) began on 19 February 1945; initially, Japanese opposition was light but as the marines moved inland the fighting became progressively intense. The island and its strategically important airfields were not secured until 26 March, but even then, isolated Japanese units held out for another three months. The covering force for the landings included no fewer than nine Essex class carriers and this formation of SB2C-4 Helldivers is from the USS *Yorktown* (CV-10), flying a support mission on 22 February. The Helldiver could carry a 1,000lb bomb in its internal bomb bay as well as a pair of underwing 500lb bombs, as shown here.

In the two weeks prior to landings on Okinawa (1 April 1945), the carriers of TF.58 launched a series of strikes against targets in southern Japan, including the important naval base at Kure on the edge of the Inland Sea. These missions were intended to reduce the ability of Japanese air and naval forces to intervene against US forces assaulting Okinawa and were followed by further strikes against other islands of the Ryukyu group. This TMB Avenger belongs to VT-6 aboard the USS *Hancock* (CV-19) and is shown over ships of TF.58 as they manoeuvre off Okinawa. The diagonal broad white stripe on the fin (and just visible on the starboard wing tip), together with the white propeller hub, are the identifying markings of the carrier's Air Group 6.

A study in US sea power in the final stages of the Pacific war. These ships are part of Task Group 58.4 on 18 March 1945, conducting strikes against the Japanese homeland island of Kyushu. Taken from USS *Intrepid* (CV-11), it shows the USS *Yorktown* (CV-10) followed by the light carrier USS *Independence* (CVL-22). A fourth carrier, USS *Langley* (CVL-27), was also present. Later that day, the task group was attacked by a force of kamikazes and both *Intrepid* and *Yorktown* were damaged but neither was put out of action. The ship in the background is the anti-aircraft cruiser USS *San Diego* (CL-53), one of three attached to the task group, which also included three battleships, two battlecruisers, a heavy cruiser and eighteen destroyers – and this was just one of the four groups that made up Task Force 58. *NHIC*

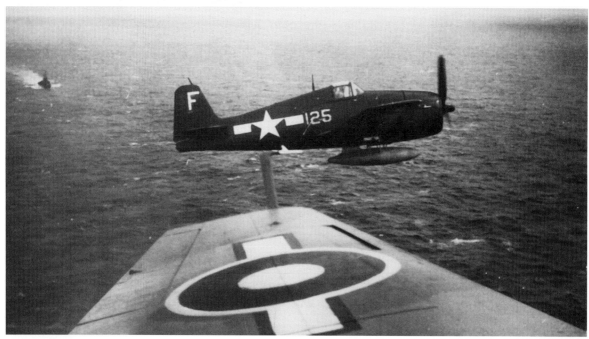

Opposite above: It was not until the summer of 1944 that Corsairs began to equip US carrier-based squadrons but the process was then accelerated from October 1944 in the face of the threat from kamikaze attacks. By March 1945, most of the fast carriers included a Corsair squadron in their air group, and this is an F4U-1D of VF-5 in the markings of CVG-5 aboard the USS *Franklin* at that time. Unfortunately, only two weeks later, on 19 March, the ship was wrecked by a Japanese attack, and although not sunk, there was a heavy loss of life and she was out of action for the rest of the war.

Opposite below: As the Fast Carrier Task Forces grew in size and complexity, the individual air groups adopted a series of distinguishing marks, mostly comprising geometric shapes such as stripes, bands, triangles and diamond patterns. At first, such markings were unofficial but by the start of 1945, the practice was so widespread that a scale of official designs (known as G markings) was promulgated for the fleet carriers and the scheme was later extended to the escort carrier groups. However, by July 1945, the sheer variety of markings was causing confusion and it was replaced by a system of prominent code letters on the tail fin, a practice that continues to this day. The F on this Hellcat in August 1945 identifies it as belonging to CVG-83 aboard the USS *Essex*. Interestingly, the photo appears to have been taken from an Avenger of the British Pacific Fleet. *AC*

In August 1944, a Grumman TBM-3 carrying an AN/APS-20 long-range radar had made its first flight. The most obvious modification was the provision of a large ventral radome while the rear and ventral turrets were removed to make way for the bulky electronic gear, all of which was controlled by a radar operator in the rear cabin. Codenamed Project Cadillac, the modified Avenger was basically a flying radar antenna and its radar signals were retransmitted down to displays on the parent ship, where they could be used by fighter controllers to direct interceptions. The appearance of the kamikaze threat in October 1944 resulted in Cadillac being given the highest priority and operational trials began using the USS *Ranger* off San Diego in May 1945. When the war ended in August, plans were underway to equip four carriers with flights of four TBM-3W Avengers in preparation for Operation Olympic.

Above: Following the final Japanese surrender on 15 August, a formal ceremony in which the surrender documents were signed by Japanese officials in the presence of representatives of all the Allied nations was held aboard the battleship USS *Missouri* (BB-63), anchored in Tokyo Bay, on 2 September 1945. Apart from the battleship, over 250 ships of the US Third Fleet and British Pacific Fleet were anchored in the bay while most of the carriers remained at sea nearby. From their decks, formations of 450 naval aircraft took off, to be joined by several hundred Army Air Force aircraft to stage a magnificent flypast over Tokyo Bay in a display of the overwhelming sea and air power that had brought the final victory. *NHIC*

Opposite: A glimpse of the future. As the war ended in August 1945, the first of the new Midway class carriers, USS *Midway* and USS *Franklin D. Roosevelt*, were almost ready to commission. They were considerably larger than the Essex class and could support an air group of over 130 aircraft. The third ship, USS *Coral Sea*, shown here with a deckload of Corsairs and Skyraiders, was not completed until 1947, although all three subsequently had long careers, including extensive involvement in the Vietnam War.

Photo Credits

Unless otherwise credited, all of the images in this publication have been sourced from the Still Images section of the US National Archive and Records Agency (NARA) at College Park, Maryland. Once again, my sincere thanks to Archive Specialist Holly Reed and her colleagues for their invaluable assistance in locating relevant images. Other images are credited as follows:

AC   Author's Collection
BPL   Boston Picture Library
LoC   US Library of Congress
NHIC   US Navy History and Information Command

Bibliography

Brown, J.D. (editor David Hobbs), *Carrier Operations in World War II,* Seaforth Publishing, 2009.

Chesnau, Roger, *Aircraft Carriers of the World, 1914 to the Present: An Illustrated Encyclopaedia,* Arms & Armour Press, 1984.

Evans, Mark L. & Grossnick, Roy A., *United States Naval Aviation 1910–2010,* US Naval History and Heritage Command, 2015.

Johnson, E.R., *United States Naval Aviation, 1919–1941,* McFarland & Co., 2011.

Kilduff, Peter, *US Carriers at War,* Ian Allan, 1981.

Lenton, H.T., *American Battleships, Carriers and Cruisers,* Macdonald & Co., 1968.

Morison, Samuel Eliot, *The Two-Ocean War,* Galahad Books, 1997.

Rohwer, J. & Hummelchen, G., *Chronology of the War at Sea 1939–1945,* Greenhill Books, 1992.

Smith, Richard K., *The Airships Akron and Makron,* Naval Institute Press, 1965.

Stern, Robert. C., *The US Navy and the War in Europe,* Seaforth Publishing, 2012.

Swanborough, Gordon & Bowers, Peter M., *United States Navy Aircraft since 1911,* second edition, 1976.

Terzibaschitsch, Stefan, *Aircraft Carriers of the US Navy,* Conway Maritime Press, 1980.

Thomas, Geoff, *US Navy Carrier Aircraft Colours,* Air Research Publications, 1989.